MOSQUES of COCHIN

പള്ളി പരിസരത്ത്
അച്ചടക്കവും,
പാലിക്കുക !

കൊച്ചിയിലെ മുസ്‌ലീം പള്ളികൾ

MOSQUES of COCHIN

Patricia Tusa Fels

C-hed
കൊച്ചി
സി-ഹെഡ്
Centre for Heritage, Environment and Development

Mapin Publishing

For M. Iqbal

1949–2007

First published in India in 2011 by
Mapin Publishing Pvt. Ltd
in association with

Centre for Heritage, Environment and Development
(Corporation of Cochin)
C-HED Building, Kacherippady
Cochin, Kerala 682 018
T: 91 484 2391766 • E: c.hed@vsnl.net

Simultaneously published in the
United States of America in 2011 by
Grantha Corporation
77 Daniele Drive, Hidden Meadows, Ocean Township, NJ 07712
E: mapin@mapinpub.com

Distributors

North America
Antique Collectors' Club, USA
T: 1 800 252 5231 • F: 1 413 529 0862 • E: info@antiquecc.com
www.antiquecollectorsclub.com

Australia & New Zealand
Peribo Pty Ltd., Australia
T: 61 2 9457 0011 • F: 61 2 9457 00228 • E: michael.coffey@peribo.com.au

Southeast Asia
Paragon Asia Co. Ltd, Thailand
T: 66 2877 7755 • F: 66 2468 9636 • E: info@paragonasia.com

Rest of the world
Mapin Publishing Pvt. Ltd
502 Paritosh, Near Darpana Academy
Usmanpura Riverside, Ahmedabad 380 013 INDIA
T: 91 79 40 228 228 • F: 91 79 40 228 201
E: mapin@mapinpub.com • www.mapinpub.com

Feroze Babu: Front Cover, 5, 6-7, 12, 18, 20, 21R, 22R, 24, 27, 29, 33, 34, 40, 41, 42, 44, 46Top, 47, 51, 53, 57, 58, 60, 61, 62, 70, 74, 80
Donald Fels: 1, 2-3, 10, 11, 15, 17, 21L, 22L, 25, 32, 35, 38, 43, 45, 46Bot, 54, 55, 64L, 69, 73, Back Cover
Krishnan Nair Studio: 9, 65
Patricia Tusa Fels: 31, 49, 64R
Maps by Shweta Bhatia Gupta

ISBN: 978-81-89995-24-9 (Mapin)
ISBN: 978-1-890206-01-7 (Grantha)
LCCN: 2008937549

Designed by Revanta Sarabhai / Mapin Design Studio
Edited by Vinutha Mallya / Mapin Editorial
Printed and processed at Thomson Press, India

Editor's Note: 'Cochin' is the colonial spelling of Kochi, a former princely state, which is now located in Ernakulam district of Kerala state. The author has preferred to retain the old spelling due to the historical context of the subject.

Front: Carved beams and woodwork at Chembitta Palli
Back: Carved gable of a building
Page 1: Mammu Surka and the adjacent pool
Pages 2–3: Life in Kochangadi, a school boy in front of Mammu Surka
Page 5: Interior of Chembitta Palli
Pages 6–7: Outer veranda at Chakarayidukku

CONTENTS

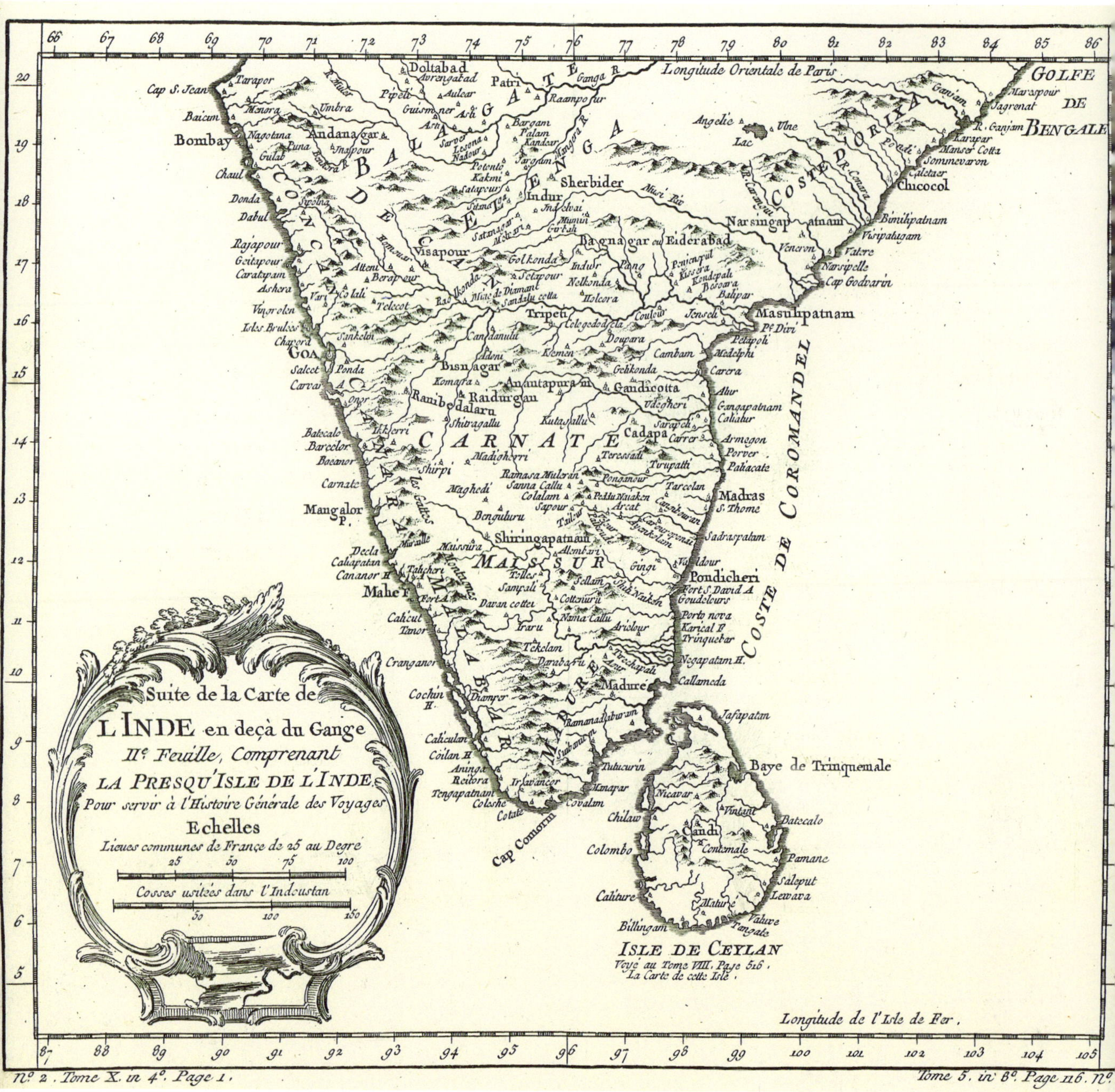

An engraved map done by J.N. Bellin in 1764 in Paris. *Source: Author's collection*

Facing page: Cochin waterway with a fleet of *thoni* delivering goods, 1950.

INTRODUCTION

"Of all the world, best is our India:
We are her nightingales and she our Garden."

Muhammad Iqbal

"Who so buildeth for God a place of worship, even if it be as small as the nest of a qata bird, God buildeth for him a house in paradise."[1]

The first contacts between the new religion of Islam and the people of India occurred peacefully, very early in the history of the faith. By the seventh century, Arab merchants had already been trading with the people of southwestern India for centuries. The exotic spices that grow along the Malabar Coast had long been objects of desire around the globe, especially pepper, the famous 'black gold'. These spices were freely traded with Middle Easterners who then carried them to Europe. Until Vasco da Gama found a sea route from the Mediterranean to India in 1498, the spice trade was dominated by Arabs who shipped spices across the sea to the Arabian peninsula. Cardamom, turmeric, ginger, cinnamon and the precious peppercorns were unloaded from ships, transported by camel overland, then sailed across the Mediterranean to

1 Inscription commonly seen at Indian mosques (found in the Hadith, a document containing stories of or about the Prophet). Another version states: "Whosoever builds a mosque for God, God will build for him a house like it in Paradise." Horovitz, J.

Cutchi Hanafi Mosque. Exterior (*left*) and ablution pond (*right*).

Italy, and from there to all of Europe. When Arabian merchants converted to Islam, they began spreading their new faith to Malabar. Learned men arrived in India to establish the faith.

With the spread of Islam came the need for houses of prayer. The mosques of Malabar are a direct reflection of the place (flat wetlands along a tropical coast with two annual monsoons), the materials (abundant wood and local stone), and the religious custom (need for a large hall for prayer). They stand as powerful and visible expressions of the integration of Islam into the culture of Malabar.

Unlike the Islamic conquerors of north India, the early Muslim traders made peace with the local leaders. The region escaped most of the invasions that swept through north India. Generations of Middle Eastern traders (Jews, Muslims and Syrian Christians[2]) arrived in Malabar with the wish to maintain the extensive, and longstanding, trading networks. There was no need for conquering warriors. For centuries, the Arabs enjoyed a golden age of Middle Eastern preeminence in trade. The native Hindu rulers welcomed all as long as they shared a common interest in cooperation.[3] This enlightened thinking brought prosperity to all.

It was only with the arrival of Vasco da Gama and the Portuguese attempt to control all overseas commerce that violence entered the trading world of Malabar.[4] From the sixteenth

2 Additional traders included north Indians, Tamils, Chinese (who abandoned their networks on the western Indian Ocean around 1430), and Southeast Asians.

3 "The Hindu rajas of the coastal states left their Muslim subjects to worship as they wished ... since the rulers' power and wealth depended almost entirely on customs revenues and the profits of their personal transactions in the maritime trade. We may suppose that the government of these cities was nothing less than a working partnership between the rajas and the leading Muslim merchants." pp. 220-21 *The Adventures of Ibn Battuta*, Ross E. Dunn.

4 "... before the arrival of the Portuguese in the Indian Ocean in 1498 there had been no organised attempt by any political power to control the sea-lanes and the long-distance trade of Asia." p. 14 *Trade and Civilization in the Indian Ocean*, K.N. Chaudhuri, Cambridge University Press, 1985.

to the nineteenth century, change swirled around the people of the coast. The Portuguese were replaced by the Dutch and then the English. The Hindu kings were partially successful in protecting the trade rights of their populace (of many different faiths) during Dutch and Portuguese reigns, but the British East India Company overpowered the longstanding, although now weakened, tradition of collaboration. During British rule, the power of the native merchants declined as the East India Company created their own exclusive trade monopolies. British 'divide and conquer' practices ultimately drove a wedge between the Hindu and Muslim peoples. These tactics were developed for the colonialists' benefit—little thought was given to the repercussions which even today haunt South Asia.

The rajas of Malabar's princely states made both peace and war with the Europeans; they also fought amongst themselves and against the invasions of inland rulers. With the loss of native people's trade income, a slow eroding of the traditions brought about by centuries of respect and peaceful co-existence began. Eventually Malabar, a series of princely states, was assimilated into the British Empire. As an old Malay proverb warned about the British arrival on Malaysia's shores: "Once the needle is in, the thread is sure to follow."

The seaside today with the Chinese fishing nets in the background.

A view of Thakyavu Palli from the water.

After the formation of an independent India, the new state of Kerala was created in 1956. Kerala, the land of lush vegetation, extensive backwaters, ubiquitous coconut trees and universal literacy, stretches along the Malabar Coast. Isolated from the rest of India for millennia by the dense forests and mountains of the Western Ghats, the people along the coastline, a thin sliver of land between mountains and sea, interacted easily with traders from all around the Indian Ocean. The sea at Kerala's doorstep brought wealth, new religions, new ideas, traders and settlers.

Midway up the coast, Cochin [now Kochi] is a jewel of the trading culture. Cochin gained ascendancy after the great flood of 1341 silted up the historic port of nearby Cranganore [now Kodungalloor]. Cochin is sited on a peninsula, with the Arabian Sea to the west, a sheltered waterway and port to the east, and the river channel's opening to the sea at the north. The natural harbour connected inland backwaters and global sea-lanes, offering a protected landing for generations of overseas traders and local merchants. After Vasco da Gama was thrown out of the northern Kerala port of Calicut [now Kozhikode] by the powerful raja, or Zamorin, the Portuguese looked to Cochin. Thus began four hundred and fifty years of European interference and eventual domination. Fort Cochin, at the northern tip of the peninsula, became the first European settlement in India, and one of the few with a history of Portuguese, Dutch and English presence. The adjacent, older settlement of Cochin (also called Mattancherry) remained the home of the ruling maharaja and site of the port. Here the storage, shipping, and trading of goods took place. As in other colonial port gateways, a multi-ethnic population learned to live and work together.

In the watery paradise of Kerala, a vast network of lakes, rivers and canals function as navigable waterways that connect the countryside to the city. Until recently, all the products of the region—spices, wood produce, rice, bamboo—arrived by *thoni* (country boats) at the portside 'godowns', or warehouses. Foreign goods arrived from China, Southeast Asia and Arabia. The Malabar coast served as an entrepôt for the Middle East and Southeast Asia, a hinge between the western and eastern ends of the Indian Ocean.

The activities of the city's older trading days have continued into the present, but in changed locales and with different rhythms. As peninsular Cochin slipped into a daydream, the mainland area of Ernakulam and the new port of Willingdon Island[5] became the centres of modern industry. Shipping containers are outlined against the huge cranes of Willingdon Island and hi-tech jobs entice the young to Ernakulam. In Cochin, the ancient commodities of rices and spices move to a different pace, at reduced volume, in and out of decaying godowns on the heads of porters. The newest 'goods' are tourists, arriving by cruise ship, airplane, train and backwater boat.

It is to Mattancherry, home to the local people, that we now turn. Here, amongst the godowns and shophouses, the Muslim community built mosques, schools, and homes. The two neighbourhoods of Mattancherry to be examined in this book, Bazar Road and Kochangadi, grew in response to the port and its commerce. These districts comprise some of the highest population densities in the present city of Kochi, and also the largest concentration of mosques. Both were trade dependent settlements, one predominantly Muslim, one a mix of many ethnic and religious groups. In both communities the patterns of town

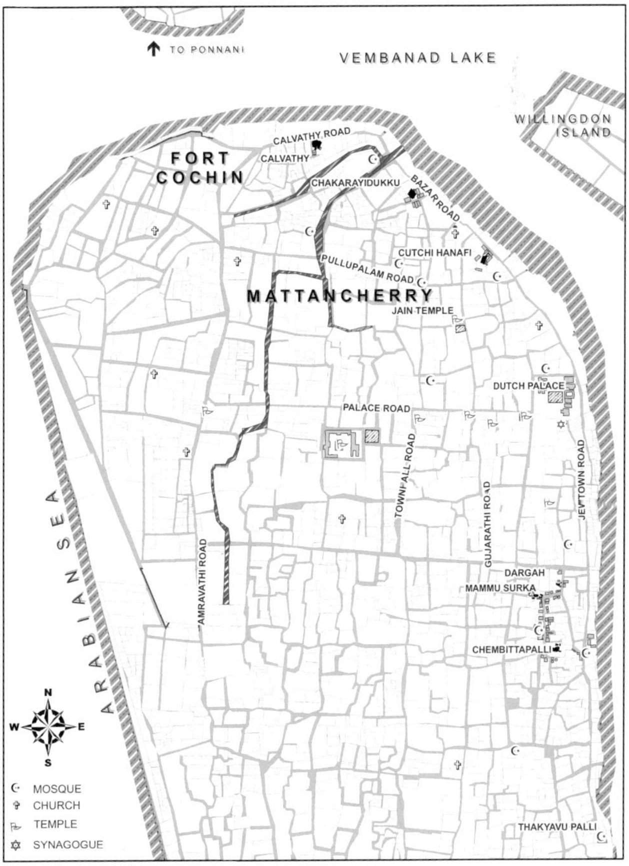

Map of the Cochin peninsula.

5 All three areas make up the modern city of Kochi.

life remain intact. With the rapid changes urban India is undergoing, these neighbourhoods are among the few that maintain physical evidence of the historic townscape. This book documents not only the mosques, but also the vibrant communities that support them.

Sited in compounds replete with coconut palms, the mosques offer an oasis of tranquility in the densely populated neighbourhoods. Large wood-framed pyramidal roofs, deep overhangs, and fine wooden craftsmanship distinguish a Kerala vernacular that reflects the climate, the culture and the materials of the place. The adoption and adaptation of the local vernacular by the Muslim congregations for their mosques is an undocumented and unappreciated phenomenon. Rarely mentioned in architectural histories or heritage surveys, the mosques' lack of recognition exposes a persistent prejudice against the humble vernacular. Recently, many of these fine old buildings have been demolished or remodelled; replaced by generic concrete structures that mirror nothing of the local history. Each of the mosque communities stewards a beloved house of worship with countless years of useful service ahead. Leaders should be encouraged in their role as custodians of an irreplaceable architectural heritage, proof of centuries of peaceful existence.

> "The past… is evidence that a society has existed. Wipe it away and a culture begins to feel, like a man without a memory, shallow and superficial."
>
> Donald Appleyard

TRADERS, SPICES AND MOSQUES

"They came to Malabar for ginger, cinnamon, arecanut, coconut, sandalwood, teak, incense, silk, cotton, ivory, jewels, and particularly black pepper…"

"What shall I say? The greatness of India is beyond description."

Bindu Malieckal

One of the many streetside traders of Kerala.

India has the third largest Muslim population in the world, after Indonesia and Pakistan. Although Gandhi stressed that India should be a secular country, religion remains a powerful force in India. For the masses of poor people religion is their guide, their community, their social life, their past, present and future. One is always aware of religion: shop owners display pictures of their god(s) or photos of Mecca. There are no secrets in the manner of faith. If someone isn't sure, they will ask. Yet, although the house of worship is a focus of people's lives, few people of Kerala would define themselves purely through religion. Faith plays a major role in their identity but is integrated into other aspects of life. It is to this balanced view that a new generation of Indian scholars is turning, noting the positive interplay between the different peoples of India that occurred in pre-colonial times. Instead of repeating the old tales of separation, they are looking to identities forged within the Indian culture, expanded and not bounded by the forces of religion.

In the times before the Portuguese arrival, the Malabar maharajas encouraged trader settlers. The Cochin raja was a patron to traders, welcoming Jews, Christians, and Muslims, Gujaratis, Tamils and Chinese. Diversity, he knew, was good for trade and trade networks. Since, traditionally, upper caste Hindus in Malabar were sanctioned against venturing out to sea, peoples of diverse faiths and faraway lands were invited into the sea-going life of Cochin. Historians have much recounted the era of peace and the pluralistic society that thrived. Prosperity in international commerce was to the advantage of everyone's pocketbook; times of economic well-being placed less stress on the social fabric. This period of tranquillity may be sometimes romanticised by local people, the rough edges removed. What is indubitable is that many take great comfort in believing that strong historical precedents exist for peoples of many faiths to live together.

At present the Greater Kochi Region (including old Cochin and modern Ernakulam) has a population of over one million with nearly 25% of that population being Muslims. Together with Kochi's concentration of Christians and Jains, the three groups come close to equaling the number of Hindus, an uncommon statistic in predominantly Hindu (80%) India. In this urban potpourri, people became more open to a multi-cultural view of themselves, identifying with their community and not exclusively with religion. Social reforms instigated after Independence by a radicalised Kerala state government, including land ownership restructuring, health care, and schooling for all, helped to create an educated, healthy citizenry.

Many of the original Muslims of Kerala came from Gujarat, Yemen and Baghdad. In seventh century Cranganore—known as Muziris in Roman times—the reigning ruler greeted Malik Ibn Dinar[1], the first Islamic leader to reach his shores, with great respect. Tradition has it

1 This date is much debated. Shaikh Ahmad Zainuddin, the 16th century author of the well known Tuhfat al-Mujahidin, claims that Malik Ibn Dinar came to Kerala 200 years after the Prophet's time, which would place his arrival in the early-ninth century.

that Malik Ibn Dinar so impressed all with his wisdom and piety that he was allotted land for a settlement. He and his followers then built what may have been the first mosques in India.

The American historian Richard White wrote about the "search for accommodation and common meaning..." People "met and regarded each other as alien, as other... over the next two centuries, they constructed a common, mutually comprehensible world." The relationship between Hindu and Muslim in Malabar was eased by the longstanding presence of Arab traders along the Malabar coast. This predisposed the local people to an acceptance of the 'other', the alien foreigner.

The spice trade, assisted by the trade winds, carried Islam to south India and southeast Asia. The Muslims of these trading ports share a distinctive faith. Traders survive and flourish because of their ability to adapt, often accommodating their religious practices to local traditions. A culture of compromise thrived, a more dynamic and flexible faith was fostered as local people voluntarily converted to the new faith while holding on to indigenous patterns. This can be clearly seen in the mosque architecture. The unique architecture of the Indian Ocean trade settlements, reflecting common climate and building materials, forms its own subset of Islamic architecture. The mosques of Kerala are some of the few remaining examples of a typology that once appeared throughout the tropical Muslim world of South and Southeast Asia. The remaining concentrations of the unique Malabar mosques can be found in the coastal cities of Cochin, Calicut and Ponnani.

Communal worship is the *raison d'etre* of any mosque. The Kerala mosque is truly a Kerala 'house' of prayer. Quite different from the mosques of the rest of India, the Malabar

Interior veranda (*left*) and exterior (*right*) of the Ponnani Juma Masjid.

mosque has been critically overlooked because of an outward simplicity. The much more elaborate stone edifices of the north have always dominated discussions of Indian architecture. Yet there is a similarity. The well known Mughal masterpieces were a result of the northern invaders slowly assimilating the influences of Indian culture; the Kerala mosques, without the invasion, likewise reflected the adaptation of local traditions.

The original mosque was Prophet Muhammad's home in Medina, a house with a large courtyard and an open portico. In Kerala, because of the monsoon rains, it was necessary to elevate the floor and provide a roof. The Prophet's open courtyard became a raised unadorned interior room. The essence of a mosque remains a positive emptiness, a space that fills and unfills, a place that marks time with the five daily calls to prayers. The composition of the Kerala mosque provided a cool, peaceful, dignified, dry, and functional place of worship.

The Arabic tradition of structural simplicity was not translated to the highly ornamental Indo-Islamic style of northern India. But the ideal of unpretentiousness married perfectly with Keralite indigenous architecture. The Malayalees[2], like all Indians, love a profusion of textures and senses, but they tended to avoid extreme displays of exuberance in their worship, food, music and buildings. This can still be tasted in Kerala food, heard in the music and seen in the older buildings by the discerning observer. Just as there is an abundance of spices available for cooking, so there was a splendid natural surrounding for buildings. Like the food, the traditional architecture integrated many elements into an ever-surprising creation. The different dishes of a meal do not overwhelm the palate but join together to produce a masterpiece; the buildings were not monumental but complemented

2 The Malayalees are the people of Kerala, Malayalam is their language.

Gable balcony at Chembitta Palli.

Prayer time settings from another era.

the lush surroundings. An outwardly straightforward geometry was based on layers of complexity; structural elements were manipulated to create harmony through balance. Except for the handsome wood carvings, the old mosques of the Malabar coast are quite austere. Local artisans adapted to Islamic injunctions against images by carving geometrical shapes, abstractions of flora, and religious inscriptions to adorn ceilings, beams, columns, doors, gable ends and eaves.

The simplicity of the mosques did not exclude timepieces and lamps, some of the few 'furnishings' of the mosques. All of the Cochin mosques display an abundance of clocks and hanging light fixtures, from hand-adjusted settings of prayer time to the latest digital product, from glass candle holders to candelabra. Often, the wall facing Mecca will have at least two clocks. All of the halls have numerous listings of the five daily prayer times. The importance of correct prayer times is reflected by the quantity of timing devices. The need for spiritual illumination is metaphorically symbolised by the array of lights.

The vernacular mosques of Mattancherry that we see today were built (and rebuilt) between the fourteenth and early-twentieth centuries. They were constructed by resident masons and carpenters, men well versed in local design idioms and methods. The mosque builders, familiar with the structure of the traditional houses and temples of Kerala, adapted these styles to create a comfortable house for prayer made of native materials. It seemed perfectly fitting that the house of prayer would respond to local customs and replicate indigenous building practices. Influences from afar are seen mainly in the details—flooring stone imported from the home country or interior particulars such as a window or door shape. As transformations in building technology occurred, some new materials or methods were incorporated into traditional techniques. Circulation of men, goods and ideas has never ceased in a port city like Cochin, even though climatic needs remained constant and cultural constraints changed very slowly.

The Kerala vernacular developed within a Hindu population and is based on spiritual tenets. But these codes of belief could be adapted in the design of a mosque. While a Hindu house should be oriented to a certain direction for the house god, the mosque *mihrab*[3] must face Mecca. All mosques are free-standing structures, oriented towards Mecca, 20 to 23 degrees north of west for Kerala. Often this causes a jog on street fronts with the rectangular form of the mosque angled to face Mecca, a clear sign to the public of the religious meaning of the building. Inside, larger mosques have a pulpit (the *mimbar)* to the right of the *mihrab*. These two elements, the focus of the praying community, are often heavily decorated and brightly painted.

3 An arched niche, the *mihrab*, marks the wall facing Mecca (the *qibla* wall). The Koran says: "We have seen the turning of your face to heaven. We shall therefore make you turn toward a *qibla* that pleases you. So turn your face toward the Holy Mosque ..."

Rooftop view of Cutchi Hanafi Mosque.

At the time of the Europeans arrival on the Indian peninsula there were three types of structures visible in Kerala: the common mud and thatch hut, more substantial houses, and religious buildings. In sixteenth century Cochin only the houses of nobles and the temples had stone walls and clay tile roofs. An exception was made for Muslim merchants who were allowed to build walls of stone. Over the centuries everyone began to build their houses with stone walls. Following a detailed science of proportion and principles of construction, the houses adhered to a hierarchy of plans: a rectangle forms the basic plan, then advances to an L or C plan, and then to the completely surrounded courtyard. The more courtyards a home had, the wealthier the owner. It was said that if a home had more than one courtyard it was the home of a nobleman. A palace was a house of many courtyards. Whereas most homes were one-storey, a two-storey home was another indicator of wealth. Two-storey homes often had a one-storey veranda that wrapped two or more sides. Religious buildings used the same structural system as the courtyard homes, albeit highly decorated. Jewish and Islamic traders based their synagogues and mosques on adaptations of vernacular plans. Interestingly the surviving Christian churches tend to show much less adherence to the local vernacular.

The house form was opened up to create a large interior hall for worship where the faithful could gather to pray. To show the importance of the building, floor heights were raised.

Left: Entry hall at Ponnani Juma Masjid.
Right: *Mihrab* and *mimbar* at Chakarayidukku, a collection of old and new light fixtures can be seen hanging from the wooden ceiling.

The old mosques were typically two-storied, although many started their lives as one-storey structures which were expanded in later centuries. Usually, one-storey verandas (or colonnades) enveloped the building to provide shaded space for discussion and/or prayer. These verandas became an important part of the composition and, as more space was needed, were often enclosed. A large front porch formed the entrance to the prayer hall, although this space was also used for prayer. The wall between the entrance and the prayer hall served as a bearing wall for second floor beams as columns disappeared from the interior. The upper floor was used for study, for visiting scholars, and for overflow crowds at Friday prayer. Many of the mosques repeated a smaller version of the *mihrab* upstairs. Balustered openings in the floor allowed the voice of the imam preaching below to reach the worshipers above.

Houses were built on a granite base, with laterite block walls, and a timber pitched roof. The walls of the mosque were also built of laterite, the porous, easily worked and abundant Kerala stone, and plastered in mud and lime plaster. A granite plinth raised the structure above the ground for protection from dampness, monsoon floods and insects. House columns were wood with a stone plinth. Mosques used wood columns and also granite, a popular variant for temples. Wooden brackets cap the columns, the more elaborate the carvings the more prestigious the building. As availability of timber changed, the shape of the mosque columns was transformed from large sculpted timbers to a simpler slimmer form. Interior posts disappeared in later mosques, with floor loads handled by beams spanning from wall to wall. The upper floors of the mosque were framed with large, exposed, squared off timbers. Joists running perpendicular to the beams combined with floor boards to create a patterned first floor ceiling. Some ceilings have a carved overlay in the form of a coffered ceiling.

At the time of the construction of these mosques, dense, insect resistant wood was abundant in the lush and luxuriant forests of Kerala. High quality timbers came out of the hills east of Cochin. Teak and beautiful jungle woods such as rosewood were transformed into eaves, air vents, columns, rafters, beams and ceilings. A long tradition of wood-working craftsmanship had developed to serve the local industries of boat and building construction. Several mosques contain inscriptions crediting a shipmaster's work. Artisan wood carvers performed their magic, replicating patterns and standards of indentation and proportion while removing any reference to temple gods.

In local vernacular buildings, wood beams and rafters displayed exact joinery. The roof developed from a simple double pitch to the gabled hip roof. Scholars are always conjecturing on what influenced a particular architectural style. Sources for the large, pitched Kerala roof are much debated: some suggest southern China, others the wood structures of Nepal, but the probable truth is that the roof form developed independently as a solution to regional conditions. The entire ensemble acted like a huge lung, allowing air in and out of the building while keeping water out. V.S. Naipaul wrote about a tropical mosque: "Much of the architectural energy of the building had gone into this roof." Construction of the signature timber roof was typical of mosques throughout the tropical areas of Asia. In the monsoon zone the motif of roof as umbrella is ubiquitous, in Kerala the umbrella has further associations with royalty and power. The grander the scale of the lofty, tiered 'crown' of the building, the more status was implied.

Exterior of mosque roof (*left*) and interior wood roof structure (*right*).

The wooden superstructure of the mosque has the most layers of complexity; beams, purlins and rafters ascending to the peak. The long standing idioms of proportion (relation of width to depth to length) and framework were faithfully followed to insure structural stability. The lack of any sag in the roofs even today speaks to the value of these parameters. Rafters were extended for overhangs to shade the walls and protect them from the weather, especially the monsoon rains. Eave boards throughout Kerala repeated standard carved details. Hipped roofs often had a gable set near the ridge; gable inserts displayed an array of floral and shaped carvings that also served as ventilation panels. Gable ends often flowered into balconies, similar to those seen in palaces, with ever-finer levels of craftsmanship. The mosques may have an ensemble of roofs, but a uniform roof pitch created a sense of balance and proportion. Early mosques employed thatch for roofing. For the well endowed mosque, copper shingles were applied over a wood base. By the sixteenth century, clay tiles had replaced the palm thatch.

There are always facilities for the ablutions obligatory before prayer. Even if one is not going to pray, the feet must be washed before entering the mosque. The washing area differs in every culture, from the fountains of the Middle East to a simple rectangular bath. In steamy Kerala the fountain was transformed into a pool; water was plentiful and washing a pleasurable and favoured activity. Malayalees could easily connect the act of washing with prayer, as Hinduism has a tradition of ceremonial bathing. The ablution pool was placed in an open veranda or an attached structure. Several mosques housed the pool in a two-storey tower adjacent to the main building. Some have adopted the courtyard tradition; the open air pool fills the courtyard space while a four-sided surround provides a roofed enclosure. Almost all of the mosques with a large pool have resident fish. Some pools are favoured by children because a caretaker will let a child catch a small fish to take home for a special occasion. Besides a source of pets, the fish also work in mosquito control, for Cochin has long been known for its abundance of mosquitoes. The pools are a reminder of another time and as mosques modernise, they are disappearing. The participants at Friday prayer no longer wish to bend down to wash and they do not want to use a common pool. Stand up fountains—similar to the one placed at Calvathy mosque during its renovation—and individual water taps are replacing the spacious, evocative pools.

Popular imagery equates a mosque with domes and minarets. Neither dome nor minaret has a liturgical imperative and neither was present in Kerala architecture. The Malabar coast had no tradition of dome building. Roof construction was of wood, not stone. The minaret developed in the crowded city, but in the villages of Kerala the call to prayer could easily reach the people. The muezzin would climb up to the roof or the second floor; now of course there are loudspeakers perched on every mosque's roof. Kerala was—and old Cochin remains—a place of one and two storied houses, villages with gardens. People believed that the height of temples should be kept below the tops of coconut palms.

Islam arrived from the Middle East, but Malayalee Muslims (children or grandchildren of converts) built their mosques using local designs and craftsmen. Today, those mosques are being torn down to be replaced by awkward copies of modern Arabic mosques or throwbacks to Mughal designs. While the mosque building is not considered sacred, the human and spiritual energy that went into the construction cannot be disregarded. It is sadly ironic that after one thousand years the local style is being discarded for an import. The lovingly crafted and sculpted roof structures are being replaced with flat rough concrete; openness to sea breezes swapped for sealed spaces. The ancient connection to the Arab world remains, for now Keralites travel to the Persian Gulf for work. Some of the returning wealth is shared with the mosques, but often these riches are misdirected. Instead of maintaining an old mosque, a new one is built or a modern expansion wraps around the old structure, making it almost invisible. After five hundred years of mosque building, the Keralites are now turning their backs to their native place, designing mosques that embrace a foreign culture. The grandeur of the old mosques with their outstanding craftsmanship and powerful spatial presence is missing in the new mosques which rely on size alone for impact.

Variations of a theme: the ablution pool at Cutchi Hanafi (*above*), the foot pool at Chakarayidukku (*following page, left*) and detail of pool at Thakyavu (*following page, right*).

Certainly, new mosques will be built as the population expands. These mosques will not look like the old Kerala mosque because the timbers are no longer available, the craftsmen are unaffordable and the styles have changed. Once the old mosques are gone they can never be replaced. Didier Repellin, a French conservation expert and UNESCO advisor on conservation, reminds us: "We have to realise that behind every detail of your beautiful heritage, there was somebody who one day gave the best of his spirit, heart and love to his work. We want to give back dignity to the qualities of human work."

The indigenous Kerala mosque architecture and the story of its growth from trade across the Arabian Sea provide a valuable historical example of cultural adaptation. Globally, there are few extant reminders of this decidedly non-violent process. The tropical mosques of the Indian Ocean are rapidly disappearing due to the forces of nature, economics and religious fundamentalism. The wooden structures of south India are some of the few survivors.

> ... "how can the separate identities of these cultures – the regionalism of Islam – survive in the face of modern views and methods that seek everywhere to standardize and unify? For the strength of Islam has always lain in unity through diversity – the unity of Islam itself through the diversity of its multifarious cultures."
>
> *Architecture in Continuity, Building in the Islamic World Today.*
> Sherban Cantacuzino, ed.

THE MOSQUES AND THEIR STORIES

"In the end, stories are what's left of us, we are no more than the few tales that persist."

Salman Rushdie

"The good storyteller tells his story... One of these mornings, the old storyteller will not wake up. But someone of those who hears his stories will tell them to others. And later this someone will also die, and the stories will stay alive as long as there are big houses and people gathered around the fire."

Eduardo Galeano

Before discussing the individual mosques, it is helpful to consider the role of stories and oral histories. All of the mosques in this book have long chronicles with uncertain and varied building dates. A sixteenth century date can be expanded back in time to the fourteenth century; one authority may claim an eighteenth century building while another puts the construction earlier. Dates in old documents refer to the Malayalam or Islamic calendar, rarely the Western calendar. For centuries there was no written history in Cochin. Even the carved inscriptions can be interpreted in various ways, some are judged illegible. The European colonialists who wrote about or documented the area barely mentioned Mattancherry, the 'native' area south of the Fort Cochin settlement. The world of the native settlement was too complicated and too 'foreign' for the Europeans.

Today, one member of a mosque gives one version of history while another recounts an altered version. The mosque we see today may have been rebuilt several times. Pieces of its past not immediately visible linger in the handed down stories.

Even the history of Islam in Malabar is given varied interpretations. Because Islam so peacefully entered the life of the coast, its early arrival was discounted by major historians. Recently, more and more research points to the arrival of Islam on Malabar's shores shortly after the lifetime of the Prophet. Logically, mosques would have been constructed from an early date. A mosque we see today may have had many antecedents, pieces of which could be visible in walls and foundations. At other sites, the remnants of older mosques have completely vanished.

In India, the Western version of historic preservation is an alien concept. Instead, until contemporary times, there was a tradition of continuity in building practices, especially as they related to religious structures. A temple could be rebuilt to maintain the spirit of the original, using the same conventions of construction. Since the materials and methods remained similar,

The imam and the muezzin at the entrance of Chakarayidukku Mosque. Imam (on right) is Abdul Rathman Haji, Mohiyadeen P.M. Abdul Majeedh has been muezzin for the last thirty years.

the resulting building was part of an on-going chronicle. It is only recently that new materials and methods have completely changed this process, resulting in a loss of continuity from ancient building to contemporary structure. Until the twentieth century, mosques were built and rebuilt on the same foundation, maintaining an ongoing presence. A mosque's past may be hidden under a series of additions or remain gloriously visible.

All that is known for certain is that the buildings hold many stories. The mosques bring physical evidence for the stories, serving as the material culture or the 'stuff' of the forbearers. They are the solid evidence for the presence of the Muslim trading communities.

Many of the old Mattancherry mosques possess an association with a Sufi scholar. The Sufi is an excellent paradigm for the architecture and the stories of these mosques. Sufis floated above Sunni and Shia sects. They enlightened with stories and embraced Hindu and Christian thought, weaving Islam into local traditions. Sufis came to teach and to convert, preaching love and tolerance. Sufis were neither Arab nor Indian or Persian, but scholars, founders and builders of community. According to an oral Sufi tradition, when a pair of scissors was gifted to Baba Farid[1], he gave it back and said, "I am not the divider but the weaver, give me thread."

On Thursdays and Sundays, the women of Cochin visit the shrines of the holy men, some of which we will examine. They come to whisper their stories, and to make requests. Since most south Indian mosques are closed to women, it is at the shrines that women can pray. The tenets of Islam make it clear that prayers should be directly to God; these women have found, in the tradition of the Sufis, a way to participate in Islam.

Fictions are added to facts, an honoured scholar added to the list of founders. Djinns (ghosts) are rumoured to be in the attic. The goal here is not to dispute stories, or to establish one shining truth. That certain stories have survived for centuries speaks to a probable basis in some facts. This is not a definitive history and it is hoped that the telling of tales will continue. In a place where names and spellings are in constant flux, physical structures adjusted constantly, and streets renamed yearly, it would be counterproductive to try and create an irrefutable classic. The variety and richness of the recountings speak to the vitality of the communities and the mosques they support. The one unquestionable fact is that the Muslim population has played a significant role in Cochin's history over many centuries.

> "Places come to exist in our imaginations because of stories, and so do we. When we reach for a 'sense of place,' we posit an intimate relationship to a set of stories connected to a particular location..."
>
> William Kittredge, *The Nature of Generosity*

> "Collective memory... is a current of continuous thought still moving in the present, still part of a group's active life, and these memories are multiple and dispersed, spectacular and ephemeral, not recollected and written down in one unified story. Instead, collective memories are supported by a group framed in space and time. They are relative to that specific community, not a universal history shared by many disparate groups."
>
> M Christine Boyer, *The City of Collective Memory*

1 Baba Farid Ganj-i Shakar was a famous Indian born Sufi (1175-1265). His shrine is located in Pakpattan, Pakistan.

KOCHANGADI

"...when any one of you enters the mosque, he should say, 'O God open to me the doors of your blessing', and when he leaves it should say, 'O God open to me the doors of your wisdom'..."

Inscription at Chembitta Palli

Carved inscription boards above prayer hall entry doors at Chembitta Palli.

South of the old Maharaja's estate (now called the Dutch Palace) and Jewtown (once home to Jewish merchants) sits Kochangadi, the original Muslim quarter. Stretching along the backwaters to the east, far from the eyes of the European colonialists who rarely travelled to Mattancherry, this area has been home to Muslims since the founding of Cochin. The settlers chose the unoccupied east side of the peninsula for its excellent harbour. Here they were protected from the rough open seas at the west. The life of the local Muslims, complete with schools, mosques, shops, storehouses, homes and shrines thrived. Today, the population remains and the five daily calls to prayer continue to fill the air, distinct voices emanating from the many different mosques.

Successful merchants built fine homes in Kochangadi and contributed to the construction of its mosques. The neighbourhood has more than a dozen mosques, catering to a predominantly Sunni population, with a variety of sub-sects and ethnic backgrounds. Coconut palms sway overhead, lush vegetation shades narrow roads, large water reservoirs bring to mind the classic Indian temple pool. Roads jog, narrow lanes branch off the main street, twisting and turning to reach groups of family homes. There are few cars on these back lanes and a village atmosphere permeates the neighbourhood. Children are everywhere, women gather to cook, to wash clothes, to talk, and to watch their offspring.

The neighbourhood is dotted with shrines dedicated to the early scholars who brought Islam to Cochin. Many are secreted in medieval lanes. One node holds the grave of Ali Marankar, a personage who, neighbours confess, they know little of except for the remembered name. An ancient banyan tree has embraced the tomb and the remnants of the shrine's stone walls.

The mosques showcased in this chapter are early adaptations of the Kerala vernacular. They are some of the oldest mosques still standing in Cochin. All sit on raised plinths of granite with plastered laterite walls. From a utilitarian foundation, the buildings rise up, each level bringing forth more finely wrought details. Door and window openings at the older mosques are rectangular; fenestration at the later structures reflects the assimilation of European influence. During the eighteenth and nineteenth centuries structural framing was simplified. Roofs continued to dominate the ensembles.

At the end of the chapter, we take a look at several mosques in Ponnani, known as the 'Mecca of Malabar'. One hundred and forty kilometres north of Cochin, the city of Ponnani is the centre of Islamic study for the state of Kerala. Here many old mosques still stand, although several have been engulfed by additions. Understanding of the vernacular mosques of Cochin can be expanded by looking at Ponnani, especially considering the strong ties that existed in the sixteenth century between the two cities. The Muslims of Cochin looked to the scholars of Ponnani for religious counsel. Both cities were active ports with large Muslim trading families, many of whom were united by marriage.

ചെമ്പിട്ട പള്ളി

Chembitta Palli—Kochangadi Juma Masjid

Malayalam: Chembu (copper) Palli (church or mosque)

The heart of Kochangadi is Chembitta Palli, the oldest and finest mosque of the area. The grand two-storey mosque is centrally located on a large plot of land. Well-travelled paths pass through the low-walled compound, connecting roads to the east, west and south. Sharing the compound with the regal mosque building are two shrines and several outbuildings. Most of the property is open, punctuated by large trees. The heavily vegetated ground is predominantly used for burial. Graveyards to the north and south of the mosque have a scattering of old granite and new marble stones. Most graves are merely body-length mounds which slowly settle back into the earth.

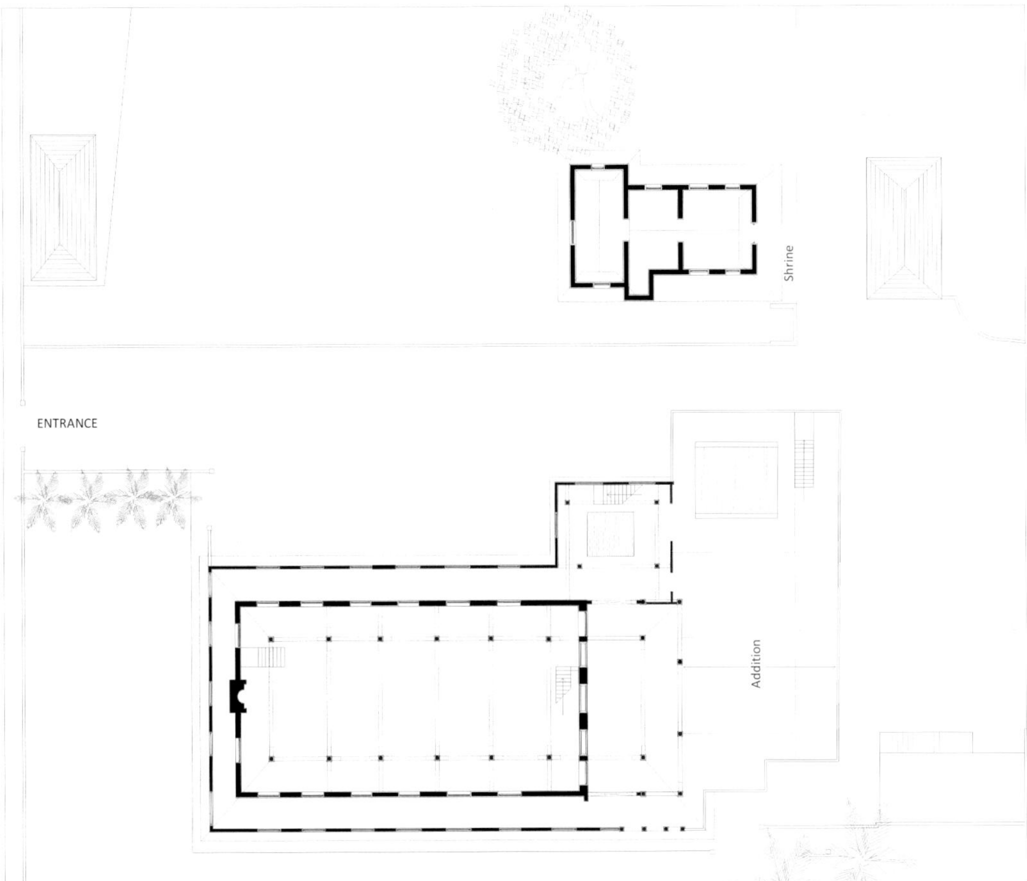

Chembitta Palli, plan and view from street entrance.

Exterior detail at Chembitta Palli.

Sometime between 1520 and 1540, the mosque that is seen today was built. Whether it was built new or built on the foundation of a smaller mosque is up for discussion. The driving force to build the mosque was the scholarly family of Sayyid Bukhari. His grave and that of his son are located in a three-chambered shrine north of the mosque. The shrine is a variant of the Kerala 'house', constructed of stone walls topped by two hipped roofs with carved gable boards.

Stories abound about the Bukhari clan. The chief figure was Sayyid[1] Ismail Bukhari, a spiritual leader of the community, who died in *hijra* 880[2]. Inscriptions date the mosque rebuilding at 926 AH. His son, Sayyid Fakhr Bukhari (or Said Maulana Bukhari Thangal) is credited with leading the construction[3]. The Bukhari clan may have originally come from Bukhara (in Central Asia), but residency on Kavaratti Island of Lakshadweep and in Kannur, an ancient trading port in northern Kerala, is also mentioned. The Sayyids, many of whom were Sufi scholars, played an important part in the teaching and conversion of Muslims in Kerala, integrating local influences and encouraging cooperation with Hindus.

Chembitta Palli is a clear visual example of this assimilation. Elements adopted from Kerala houses and temples define the architecture of the mosque. Known carvers and artisans

1 A Sayyid was said to be a descendent of the Prophet, but Sayyid can also be a term of respect.

2 Muslim years are counted from the date of the hijra (the Prophet Muhammad's journey from Mecca to Medina), July 622 AD. Hijra dates will be shown with AH.

3 "mosque was reconstructed by Said Maulana Bukhari Thangal who came from Kavarathy in the Hijara year 926" (City document). In Kerala the name Thangal (or Thangel) refers to a respected person or, some say, an ancestor of the prophet.

Woodwork at Chembitta Palli. Carved rafters at second-floor louvers (*left*); Close up of the *qibla* wall (*right*).

Prayer hall at Chembitta Palli.

were brought from nearby areas to help build the new mosque. Records at the mosque also mention boat builders, who were well versed in woodwork. In order to position and join the sizeable beams and columns of Chembitta Palli, a knowledge and skill in working with large timbers would have been essential.

The imam of the last forty four years, Al-Haj K.K. Abdul Rahiman Moulavi, tells a story that has been passed down about the timber that was used for the mosque: A local Jewish merchant was so impressed with the knowledge of the Sayyid that he wanted to help in the building of the mosque. He donated all the timbers.

Some embroider this story by telling how the Jewish merchant then decided to convert after hearing the erudition of the Sayyid's sermon on Moses.

The second-floor structure, the two-tiered roof structure and all of the columns are wood. Impressive main floor columns support the beams for the upper floor and carry the load of the roof structure to the ground. At the second floor, the columns extend up to the beams and rafters of the high roof. All of the wooden superstructure elements are notched to fit together tightly. Each column has been shaped from a single timber into alternating geometrical sections (square and octagonal), a common motif in the stone columns of south Indian temples as well as the wood pillars of Kerala palaces.

Imam Al-Haj K.K. Abdul Rahiman Moulavi.

An original colonnade encircled three sides. It was later enclosed with a series of shuttered openings which aligned with the interior openings, thus maintaining the light and airy feel of the interior. Inside the colonnade and at the space between interior columns and the original outside wall, the sloping rafters of the lower roof can be seen.

A gracious large entrance porch fronts the main prayer hall.

Above the prayer hall doors are wood panels with carved inscriptions. The porch ceiling displays wood coffering, a device often seen in buildings of importance. The structure of the entrance porch matches that of the main hall, with the sloped rafter space wrapping three sides. The ceiling coffering has been stained a dark deep brown, in contrast with the white of the upper structure of the main hall.

The prayer hall has a single *mihrab* centred on the *qibla* (west facing) wall; this projection is not visible from the exterior because the veranda extends across this side. To the right of the *mihrab* sits the wooden *mimbar*. Very few wooden pulpits remain in Kerala and this one is an excellent example of wood carving skills of that time.

The second-floor has a smaller footprint than the first as the walls align with the main floor columns. The space has a high open ceiling. Louvers angle outward from bottom to top— a traditional Kerala style found in palace architecture and temples. Used for study and rest, the chamber also serves as an annex for Friday prayer. A flight of steep stairs leads from the main hall to the upper floor. The upper roof of the mosque is covered with flat copper shingles—thus the

Shrine of Sayyid Bukhari on the grounds of Chembitta Palli.

name of the mosque. The hipped roof has one exterior gable facing east, above the old entry. The gable takes on a balcony form with columns and balustrades, all elaborately carved in the quintessential Kerala style.

In Cochin today, there is little of such a substantial nature that dates back almost five hundred years. The building of the mosque was a major undertaking and proof of the success of the Muslim traders, their optimism, and their commitment to their community. Wealthy traders contributed funds while less affluent members of the community donated their own labour to the building project.

The mosque community includes twenty-two hundred families. During Friday prayer, attendees overflow the original hall. Because of this, in recent times a concrete flat-roofed hall was built to the east along with a large ablution pool. An older two-storey annex, north of the main hall, houses the smaller, original pool. These assemblies are the only additions to the original mosque. Unfortunately, the concrete hall blocks a view of the primary entrance porch and its decorative gable.

As the community grew, an additional prayer mosque was built to the east. A lane connects the prayer mosque (Mahallara Palli) with Chembitta Palli's east gate. The mosque has a dominant presence on the street as the entire westerly (*qibla*) wall protrudes into Kochangadi Road. Since it is located literally in the street, there are no porches or verandas on the two exposed sides. Mahallara Palli, a seventeenth or eighteenth century two-storey construction, has a great majestic roof which easily competes with the large seaside godowns that march along the road.

മമ്മു സുർക്ക പള്ളി
Mammu Surka

Within calling distance of the one-and-half acre compound of Chembitta Palli are several other old mosques in the Kerala vernacular; some are Friday mosques[4] and others are smaller prayer mosques. Mammu Surka is a prayer mosque, the congregation attends Friday prayer at Chembitta Palli.

The area between the two mosques is home to several large pools. Across from Chembitta Palli sits Andam Kulam (annual death pool). Tradition has it that at least one person would drown in the pool every year. Generations of children have been advised to stay away and supposedly accidental drownings no longer occur. Two-hundred metres north, another pool forms part of the property of the Mammu Surka mosque. This tank, along with Andam Kulam, marks the probable site of ancient springs which were enlarged for a community water source. Both tanks are still used for washing by local people.

Mammu Surka is reached from the street by a small lane. Like the lanes at Chembitta Palli, this walkway serves as an east–west passage. A madrasa located on the second floor of a narrow building bordering the lane has shops on the lower floor. To the left, and to the right behind the madrasa building, open space is utilised for a burial ground, complete with a grove of mature mango, jackfruit and coconut trees.

---

4 Mosques that hold the major prayer or sermon of the week are called Juma Masjid (Friday mosques). They always have a pulpit (*mimbar*) for the imam to deliver his weekly sermon whereas small mosques which do not hold Friday midday service have no mimbar and are used only for daily prayers.

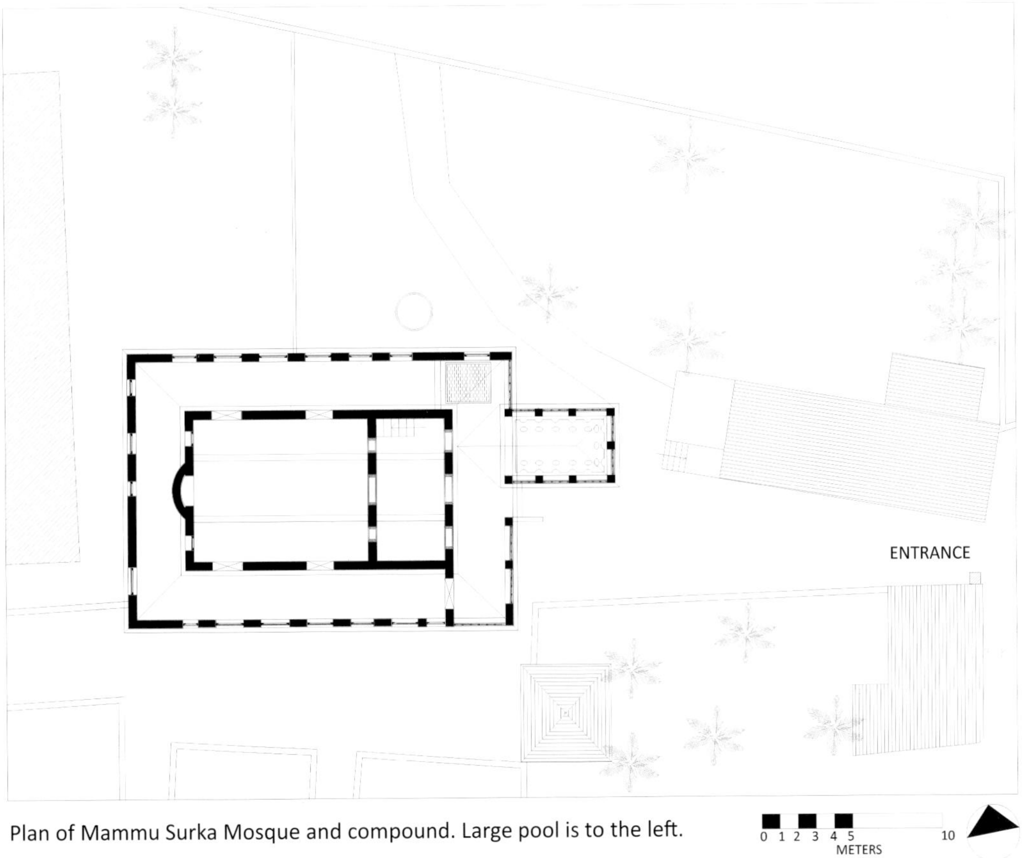

Plan of Mammu Surka Mosque and compound. Large pool is to the left.

The mosque was built by Mammu Surka (or Sarka), a member of the Naina family. The Naina family, privileged members of the king's court, was also connected to Chembitta Palli. Some say they served as tax officers for the Cochin raja. Inscribed over the main entry door is the name Masjid Al Hadhadi Al Alavi, the official name given to the mosque by the builder. But the name of Al Hadhadi Al Alavi, who was a famous scholar, never had common usage among the community who prayed at the mosque. The mosque remains under the care of the Naina family; Haji Kutty Naina is the present *muthavalli*[5]. Funding for the operation of the mosque comes from the rent of seven small shops on the property and the harvesting of ten coconut trees.

Construction dates for the mosque are sketchy. An agreement detailing ownership and maintenance was registered with the government in 1834. By then, the mosque had already been functioning for some time and the personage noted as Mammu Surka may have been the grandfather of the agreement maker.

5 The *muthavalli* is the administrative head of the mosque, usually a descendent of the founder.

Details of the mosque: Prayer hall, entry porch and ablution seats.

Although everyone agrees that the builder was of the Naina family, stories abound about the name Mammu Surka. Some say the name comes from Mansur-ika, *ika* signifying a respected elder and Mansur a well known ship captain. Others say that the founder was a rich business man from Mysore: Mysore-ika.

The style and construction of the mosque date it to pre-nineteenth century. The exterior of the structure exhibits the modest outlines of a Kerala house. The interior displays the typical planked and beamed ceiling, with no columns in the main prayer hall. Rectangular doors and shutters are of plain wooden construction. Door frames repeat the classic detail of Kerala columns: squared-off edge alternating with angled edge (source of the octagon shaped column). The two-storey prayer hall has a hipped terracotta roof, balanced by the one-storey veranda roof. The veranda wraps all four sides of the building. A single-storey ablution area completes the composition.

Moving away from the temple-influenced design of Chembitta Palli, the mosque is an example of the evolution to a simpler Kerala mosque, reflecting the loss of the great fortunes of earlier times. This style of mosque was repeated up and down the Malabar Coast for centuries. Having undergone no alterations, its integrity intact, Mammu Surka is an excellent example of this period.

ഷൈഖ് സൈനുദ്ധീൻ മഖ്ദൂമിന്റെ ദർഖ

Dargah of Shaikh Zainudheen Makhdoom

As the road turns to the east, the cherished shrine (dargah) of Zainudheen Makhdoom (or Makhdum) appears. Shaikh Zainudheen came from Yemen in the fifteenth century and settled in Cochin where he became a well known teacher and spiritual leader. There might have been a connection between the Shaikh[6] and an original mosque at Chembitta Palli. His son Ali was an important figure in the religious life of Cochin. Future generations of the family included Shaikh Zainuddin[7] Makhdum Abu Yahya, who authored many religious books and witnessed the arrival of the Portuguese, and Shaikh Ahmad Zainuddin, the well known author of *Tuhfat al-Mujahidin* (1583), a history of south Indian Muslims and the devastation inflicted by the Portuguese. Abu Yahya, known as Zainuddin I, was born in 1467 in a small house adjacent to the shrine, now a madrasa.

The shrine shares a compound with Akathe Palli[8]. The original Akathe Palli dated from the late-sixteenth century, but was demolished several years ago. The floor and base remain; a new mosque with no outside veranda was built on the old footprint. All of the timber roof structure is gone. A concrete framed, flat-roofed structure has been inserted into the space west of the shrine; the original ablution pool sits to the north. The tombs of the Shaikh and his granddaughter Zainaba Bibi are housed in a tiny house with carved rafters and gable end. The finely carved inscription panels that once filled part of the triangular space at the gable have disappeared. The two-roomed shrine has an entrance room and the tomb chamber. Built long after the death of the Shaikh, evidence from inscriptions places the date of construction of the shrine and the original Akathe Palli in the late 1590s.

---

6 *Shaikh* refers to an elder, or a respected Islamic scholar.

7 Zainudheen (also Zainuddin) is a popular name in Kochangadi and is the local spelling for the Arabic Zain al-din. More about Abu Yahya can be read in the section on Ponnani mosques. The Ponnani branch uses the Zainuddin spelling.

8 Akathe in Malayalam refers to an inside room or 'a little bit inside'.

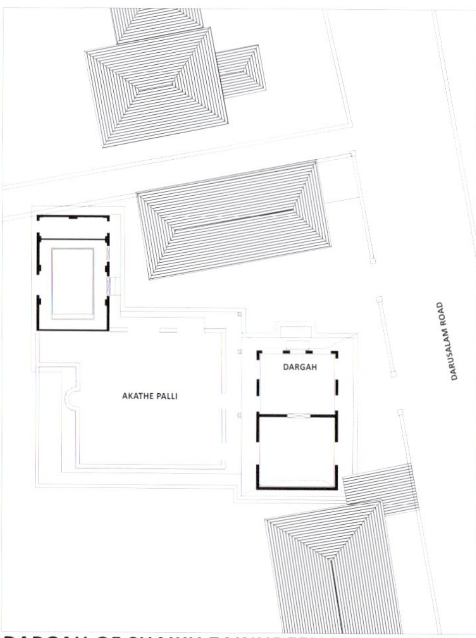

DARGAH OF SHAIKH ZAINUDEEN MAKHDOOM

0 1 2 3 4 5 10 METERS

Interior of shrine (*top*), plan of shrine and mosque (*below, left*), exterior view of shrine with the newly constructed Akathe Palli to the right (*below, right*).

There is some disagreement in the records as to whether the tomb houses Ali ibn Zainudheen or his father Zainudheen. What is certain is that the family came from Mahabar in Yemen (some say the word Malabar came from the Arabic Mahabar) and that the family had many famous Islamic scholars. There is also no doubt that they were connected to Ponnani, which the local people call the 'Mecca of Kerala'. Ali's son Abu Yahya built (or rebuilt) the Juma mosque in Ponnani and there was an obvious dialogue between the mosque builders of the two towns. The title of Makhdoom (Arabic for holy servant) was conferred on descendents of Zainuddin—the present Makhdoom is the fortieth—who are officially the keepers of the Juma Masjid in Ponnani.

Dargahs are considered abodes of peace, offering calm and blessings. This shrine continues to be popular with the women of Kochangadi. Like others in the area, it is tended with care and displays the quotidian offerings of the community.

തക്യാവ് പള്ളി
Thakyavu Palli

Malayalam: Thakyav (small)

Moving further south there is one more mosque of note. A fishing community that flourished in this area built several mosques; all of the original mosques have been replaced with twentieth-century structures, except for Thakyavu Palli. With the entrance facing the backwaters, the mosque sits in a large compound which also includes a shrine, a madrasa, and several family homes built in traditional Kerala style.

Entrance to Thakyavu Palli, the front veranda faces the backwaters.

The mosque has always been associated with a Thangel family who emigrated from Ponnani at the invitation of the Cochin raja.[9] There are Thangels all over India, but in Kerala they were known as spiritual leaders. The original Thangels came from the Arabian peninsula.

Hashim Kochukoya Thangel, the present leader, lives in the compound and tells the story of the founder, Sayyid Abul Backer Bumb. The Sayyid's father called him Bamb, which comes from the Malayalam word *vambon* meaning 'strong in the brain man'. Abul Backer was

9 Francis Day wrote that the chief priest resided in Ponani and was called 'Tungel'.

Exterior of Thakyavu Palli: two-storey portion is the shrine of Abul Backer, prayer hall is at right.

Interior view, ablution area.

a well respected teacher who lived and died (in 1229 AH) at Thakyavu, and is buried in the shrine, along with his brother and his brother's son. People come from all over Kerala and also Ceylon—where Abul was also well known—to leave offerings at his tomb. Bumb's father, Sayyid Abdul Rahman Hydrose lived from 1099 to 1164 AH (died 1751 AD). He was a known scholar and the madrasa at the site is named for him. Hydrose, whose family originated in Yemen, came to Malabar in the beginning of the eighteenth century (1115 AH), supposedly from Surat, Gujarat where he had been previously residing.

View of the prayer hall from the entrance of Thakyavu Palli.

The present mosque was probably built in the early nineteenth century, during Abul Backer's lifetime. Granite stones pave the entry to the mosque which has three connected sections: the shrine—a two-storey structure, the two-storey prayer hall, and the ablution pool building. The steep pitched roofs of the three sections define the building, along with a series of squat stone columns across the front of the mosque and pool. The columns are made of a granite-like stone brought from Gujarat. The enclosed verandas of the earlier Kochangadi mosques are not present, except at the front porch. Instead, Thakyavu has bracketed roof overhangs, an element which appears in several of the Bazar Road mosques. The prayer hall has rectangular windows with fanlights, a nineteenth century addition to the Kerala vernacular. The entire ensemble is painted a delicious pink with lime-green trim.

Ponnani

A short excursion north from Cochin is necessary to better comprehend the ubiquitous Kerala mosque. Up and down the Malabar coast traders made connections, families intermarried, and Islam spread. While each mosque has its unique history, all of the mosques display the shared traditions of wood and stone construction and a commonality of form and massing derived from the religious need for communal prayer.

Ponnani, a Malabar port city inhabited from the first century AD, was a religious centre of temples and mosques. Here can be found an ancient mosque, Thottungal Palli (or Kadavu Palli[10]). Some believe that its founding can be linked with Malik Ibn Dinar, who built ten

10 *Thode* is Malayalam for canal side; *kadavu* means jetty. A canal used to connect the mosque to the river, but the river moved and is now directly at the mosque's feet, along with the jetty for the river crossing ferry.

Exterior gable at Thottungal Palli.

mosques in the area around Cranganore. Others state that Thottungal Palli was built in 1200 by Shaikh Fareedhudheen and his student, Shaikh Hussein. Since Shaikh Hussein's tomb is located at the mosque, this claim may have more validity. All agree that Thottungal was the main mosque of the town until the big Juma Masjid was built in the early 1500s. Considering the mosque's long role in history, it is all the sadder that both, this and Malik Ibn Dinar's mosque at Cranganore, have been encased in concrete additions. In 2008 construction was underway at Thottungal Palli; all of the verandas were gone, replaced by flat roofed extensions, and a dome was being built at the waterside. The main prayer hall and entry remain. Both are simple open rooms with no interior columns. The structure and form indicate the beginning of the Kerala mosque style. The roof and balcony gable also remain, complete with a fantasy of decorations.

Not far from Thottungal stands the Juma Masjid of Ponnani. Construction of the mosque began sometime between 1510 and 1519 and was completed before the death in 1522 of Abu Yahya (Zainuddin I), the founder of the mosque and grandson of Shaikh Zainudheen of Cochin. Abu Yahya was an influential man in the Kerala Islamic community. Besides founding many mosques in Ponnani he also wrote religious treatises, some of which are still used. He is buried in a tomb adjacent to the mosque entry.

Grand entrance gable and balcony of Ponnani Juma Masjid.

One of the many stories about the mosque's founding goes like this: "A Hindu merchant and a Muslim merchant travelled across the sea with trading goods. When a large storm appeared in the sea they realised their lives were in danger. If they survived and got to land, the Hindu promised to build a temple, the Muslim to build a mosque. The travellers survived and the ship landed on Ponnani beach. One built the Juma Masjid and the other the Thrikavil Bagavathy temple. If you walk east from Juma Masjid for eight minutes you will reach the Thrikavil Bagavathy temple."

Although construction began in the same period as Chembitta Palli, the Juma Masjid of Ponnani differs in several ways. Instead of the interior wooden columns of Chembitta Palli, the Ponnani prayer hall has a series of majestic arches coming down to stone columns. Both mosques have gable porches, but the one at Ponnani is more elaborate than Chembitta Palli's. The second floor at Ponnani is a full floor with a third floor attic above and all floor heights are greater than Chembitta Palli. There is also disagreement about the date of the Juma Masjid that we see today. The sixteenth-century original, which historical documents cite as 'ninety feet long and sixty feet wide' (as it is today), was renovated in 1753–54. It may have been expanded upward with a more elaborate gable balcony and attic at that time. Chembitta Palli maintains its

Entrance porch.

Ablution pool.

Carving at the wooden mimbar.

Third floor of the mosque.

sixteenth-century composition. Also, some records indicate that the mosque was burned by the Portuguese in 1550—although the extent of the damage is not clear. Similarities between the two mosques include large gracious and decorated entry halls with coffered ceilings, finely carved wooden *mimbars*, handsome inscription boards, and colonnades. Both mosques also share unsympathetic additions at the gable end. At Ponnani, a clutter of additions shield the great front. Each new structure has taken on a different style; an Arabic turret, a Kerala gable, Middle Eastern mini-domes and modern cement curlicues.

Sixteenth-century mosques like Ponnani's Juma Masjid and Chembitta Palli are manifestations of the power, wealth and prestige that resided in the community. The fantastic displays of these mosques may be a direct response to the Portuguese efforts at destruction of the Muslims' trade dominance and their faith. According to legend, several mosques were burned to the ground. Zainuddin I was a force who reinvigorated the population, rebuilding mosques, writing religious treatises, penning freedom songs and encouraging the Muslims to continue in their faith.

BAZAR ROAD

"On reaching the Muttencherry bridge, which crosses a sluggish canal, ... boats are generally seen in the afternoon, bringing in fish, oysters, and vegetables for sale. On its further side the bazaar may be said, really to commence. ... shops are seen on either side of a narrow street, and before many of them, the salesman is seated on the ground, with his merchandise spread out around him. Here is the fruiterer, with piles of pumpkins, bandikyes, pine-apples, guavas, chillies, and other vegetable productions; whilst next door, there are live monkeys, of both black, and brown varieties, a mongoose or two, with parrots, loris, mynahs, and pigeons. Again there is an herbalist's, where the votaries of native drugs, procure the necessary ingredients, the smoker his tobacco, the opium eater his accustomed stimulus, the bhang consumer the dose which gives him such delicious reveries, and the betel chewer the leaf wherein he wraps pieces of chunam, with the nut of the Arcca palm, ... The petty Hawker seated by the side of the street, is loudly proclaiming the praises of his wares."

Francis Day

Overflowing with trucks, carts, pedestrians, head-carriers, bicycles, motorbikes and cars, Bazar Road links Fort Cochin to Mattancherry (Francis Day's Muttencherry). Bazar Road was the heart of the native part of town, the bustling bazaar of the region. Here a great mix of people resided: Arabs, Gujaratis from the north, Tamils from the east coast, Afghanis, Pakistanis, traders from Bombay, Christians and Jews from the Middle East, and, of course, Malayalees. At the southern terminus of Bazar Road sits a complex that includes the Maharaja's Palace and a Hindu temple. Within a kilometre radius can be found Hindu temples, numerous mosques, a Jain temple, a Jewish synagogue, a Catholic church, Syrian Christian shrine, and to the south Kochangadi, the Muslim medieval quarter. All of the diverse people of Mattancherry were brought together repeatedly during years of living and working in close proximity. Over time, immigrant groups assimilated the ways of Kerala and those of their fellow citizens into their own customs. Everyone became less exclusive or self-defined and more cosmopolitan.

Godowns full of rice, rubber, spices, cashews, hardware, and plastic goods line the street and stretch eastwards to the water and the port. Delineating the east edge of the roadway are grand warehouses with imposing double doors leading to expansive courtyards which extend to the water's edge. For centuries this was a place of exchange, a locus for movement of people and goods, a hub for the products that had propelled men to voyage great distances. Cochin became a marketplace for the desired goods of peoples from Beijing to Amsterdam. Today, looking at the empty wharves it is hard to imagine that once this waterway was packed with boats. Even thirty years ago, one could 'walk' the water's edge by jumping from one boat to another.

Mammuka in his tea stall.

One of the ubiquitous tea wallahs of Bazar Road, Mammuka, told what he had seen over the last sixty years. A man of eighty, he works in a tiny blue shack where he has boiled up tea for generations. "Bazar Road was a great trading centre, Cochin a great port where all the companies of America and Europe sent freighters. But from about twenty years ago [or after the 1970s], the trade is disappearing. Why? The politicians and the trade union heads have destroyed the port. They asked for too much money. They have forced the trade to go elsewhere. Before Independence the British were big, and merchants from Karachi and Kutch who came to trade. A Karachi family called Alai were the biggest and the wealthiest. But they left and returned to Pakistan after Partition. Besides rice, produce and spices, gold and textiles were traded on this street—all came here. There was no business in Ernakulam. Now there is no business here."

On the roads leading inland, ethnic communities long connected to trade have maintained their own unique historic enclaves. Thirteen different linguistic groups can still be found in Cochin. Walking through Mattancherry one crosses a street and moves from the communities of one state of India to another.

In the midst of this linear, dense streetfront, mosques can be reached through lanes between shops or, in the case of the Calvathy Mosque, face directly on to the busy street. Here the men of the community, just metres away from their work, have a place to pray or rest. For the most part, the mosques of Bazar Road are more recent than those of Kochangadi. The area developed into what we see today in the late-eighteenth and early-nineteenth century. The British had established themselves, Gujarati merchants were building permanent warehouses, and quantity of trade was increasing. Here we can see the next stage in the mosque development, reflecting new influences from both the Gujaratis and the Europeans. Arched openings and fanlight windows were integrated into the Kerala model; the Kerala roof held steady, along with the basic floorplan and construction methods.

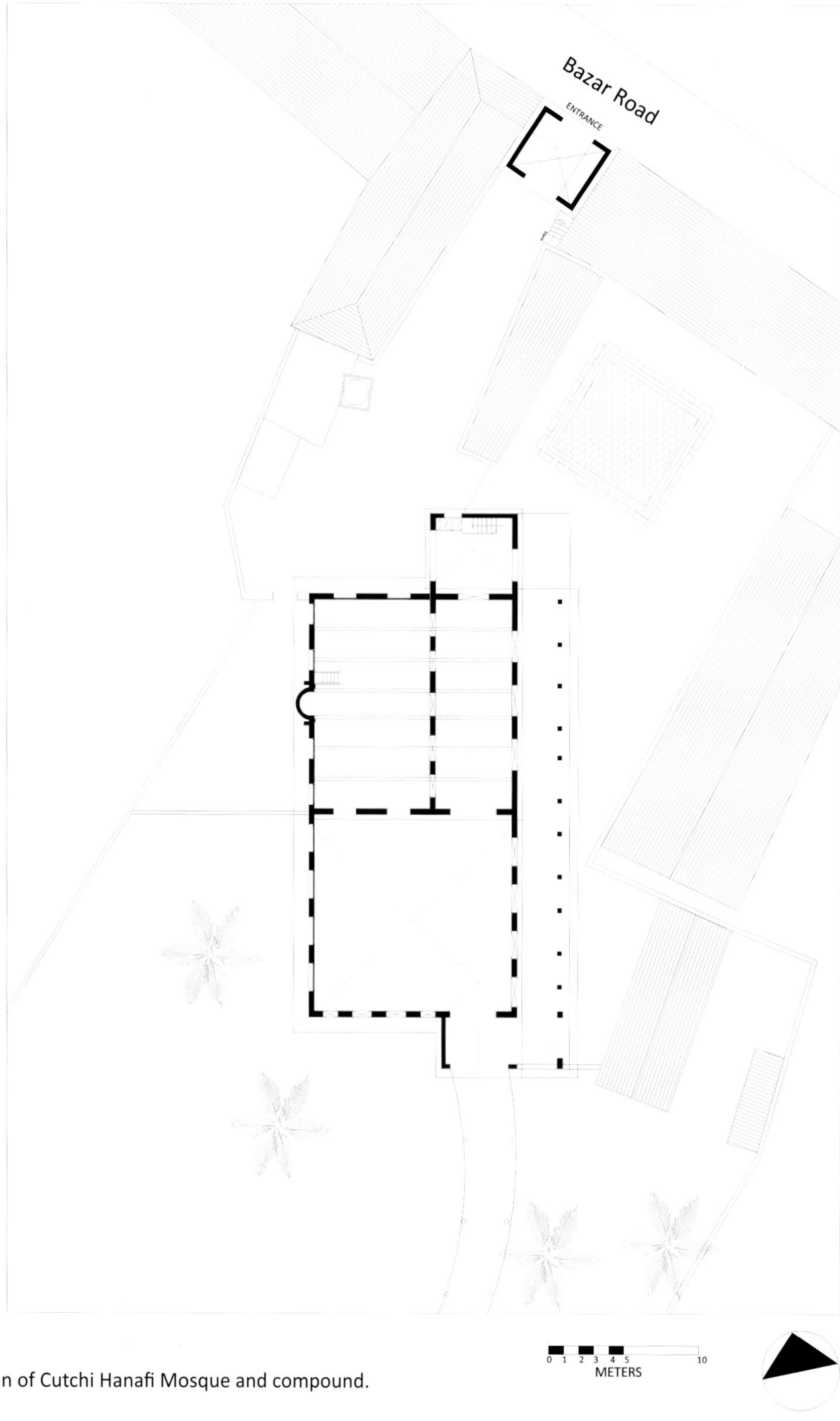

Plan of Cutchi Hanafi Mosque and compound.

കച്ചി ഹനഫി പള്ളി

Cutchi Hanafi Mosque—Cutchi Memon Hanafi, Cutchi Pazhaya Palli

Malayalam: Pazhaya (old)

Perched on the western edge of Gujarat state the district of Katchchh (formerly Kutch) sits on the Pakistan border. An arid terrain, the land is flanked by salty marshes and the Arabian Sea. From here, many men set out to sea. Known for their trading abilities, Gujaratis had contacts with Arabia, China and throughout India. Gujarati textiles were sought after throughout the Middle East and Southeast Asia, where they were even used as a medium of exchange for spices.

From the early trading days of Cochin there has been a Gujarati presence. Part of that large community includes the Cutchi Memons (Sunni Muslims) and the Jain Gujaratis who speak the Kutchi dialect. It is said that the King of Cochin offered land for settlements—as he did for the Jewish community—to the Cutchi Memons (or Kutchi Memons) because of their renowned trading abilities.

Tradition has it that in 1819 a massive earthquake hit the Kutch region. The fertile agricultural land became laden with salt, the freshwater disappeared. At this time a huge

Congregation in the prayer hall at Cutchi Hanafi mosque. The hall has ornate plaster work at the arched *mihrab* and original lighting at the beamed ceiling.

migration of the Cutchi occurred. The majority moved to Bombay or to Cochin, places known through their longstanding trade connections.

Javeed Hashim, a third generation Cochin Cutchi, tells a different story about their migration:

"They say the earthquake brought the Cutchi here. I have another story about them. There was a Cutchi king who was very powerful and who loved women. Every time he saw a beautiful woman he told her to come live at his palace. He would be riding through the streets or countryside and see someone and want her. One day a group of cowherds came through: cows, men, women, and children. The king saw amidst them a very beautiful woman. He wanted her. But when he said something to her she said she had no interest in coming to his palace and that she was married. The king went and found the archers in his army and he dispatched them. They went and killed all the cows and men. The beautiful woman was very upset. The king said she should come and live with him. When they made the pyres to burn the bodies, the beauty jumped on her husband's pyre and called out curses on the king and his kingdom: may the land dry up, your offspring die, the waters recede."

Since their arrival in Cochin, the Cutchi have prospered; there are now over three thousand community members. Besides trading in spices and cloth, they were successful in 'transshipment', importing and exporting goods from Cochin. They also branched out into seafood, hotels, and construction. In 1898 they established the Indian Chamber of Commerce. Known for their philanthropy, the Cutchi have founded charitable trusts to fund schools, healthcare, and orphanages. They also own sizeable amounts of property on Bazar Road where they continue to subsidise rent for many marginal businesses. The community originally lived only around Bazar Road, but since the 1950s they have spread throughout greater Cochin so that now there are eighteen Cutchi mosques.

In 1815 the Cutchi Memon community decided to build a mosque on Bazar Road. Stories suggest settlement in Cochin before this date, there may have been a first mosque with a thatch roof. But the mosque that we see today was built between 1815 and 1825. The first imam of the present mosque was Haji Ibrahim Bawa, a Sufi scholar who came from Gujarat in the early nineteenth century. The mosque was built by Haji Dosal Kadwani Sait, a wealthy, successful Kutch merchant. It is now managed by an organisation—Cutchi Memon Jamath[1], which also owns several adjacent properties. The rent from these shops and buildings is utilised for the operation of the mosque.

An arched entry gate leads from hectic Bazar Road down a small lane to the peaceful compound of the Cutchi Mosque. The original mosque is a fourteen-metre-square, two-storey

1 The Memons are descendents of the Lohana community of Sind who converted to Islam; those who settled in Kachchh were called Cutchi Memons.

structure with a large hipped roof. The building displays elements of the local vernacular and relates directly to a class of formidable streetfront warehouses lining Bazar Road, although the detail and ornamentation is much more refined in the mosque. Many of the extant Bazar Road structures were built in the early 1800s by Guajarati merchants to replace the thatch huts which previously lined the road.

Entrance to mosque from Bazar Road.

The prayer hall is a single room with no columns, extending into a generous entry hall through five large arched openings. Two archways at the south open into the 1840 addition, a square one-storey structure for burial functions. The designer of the mosque incorporated elements from the Kachchh vernacular: the prevalence of arches and the curved plaster details remind worshipers of their homeland. Elegant carved four-panel doors are a profusion of ovals; this oval is then repeated as one single element on the inside of the wood shutters, a favoured detail from Kachchh repeated on many of the Bazar Road warehouses. The *mihrab* arch displays a cornucopia of leaf and flower designs rendered in plaster. The level of detail confirms the presence of skilled local artisans who were found to work with the resident craftsmen. After the massive 2001 earthquake in Kachchh destroyed many ancient buildings, some say these details can now only be found here.

Six substantial wooden beams span across the prayer room. The original glass bell jars which held candles still hang from the beams, along with their successor candelabra. Openings to the exterior have fanlights with colored glass above wooden shutters. The glass is believed to be original; a mix of blue, green, red and clear panes set into the fanlight frame. The wooden balusters at the lower portion of the window openings are made in the classic Kerala style as is the exterior eave board. From the outside, the rounded bay formed by the arched interior *mihrab* can be seen on the *qibla* wall.

The space upstairs is completely open and presently unused. This space has balustered openings in the floor and a small *mihrab* for the overflow crowd that formerly utilised the second floor. The wooden tie beams and roof structure are exposed and replicate the ubiquitous Kerala roof. The steepness of the roof creates an expansive, prominent presence, calling out the public function of the building.

Unlike the older mosques of Kochangadi there is not a covered veranda with columns surrounding the building, but instead a braced overhang roof at the first floor. Off the entry hall,

Entry veranda.

Walking from the ablution area to the exterior courtyard.

Qibla wall of the mosque.

Granite water holder.

a veranda with wood columns extends along the entire southeast side of both prayer room and burial space. There is an expansive ablution pool, almost eight-metre-square, adjacent to the veranda. At the east corner of the mosque a two-storey tower serves as entry, foot pool, and stair for the second floor.

The floor at the entry and along the veranda is of granite pavers. These, along with several large water holders each carved from a single piece of granite, were all imported from the Kachchh region. One stone vessel sits adjacent to the ablution pool, three sit along the entry path, adjacent to the old well and a series of vaulted bathing rooms. Long ago, water from the well would be placed in the vessels for bathing. An assistant would pour water over the bather, while sometimes also heating the bath water.

The compound is large, with an extensive unbuilt area set aside for burial. Besides the Bazar Road entry, a path to the west leads to the residential area. Coconut palms proliferate, providing generous shading around the building and cemetery area. Surrounded on all sides by the densely built up area of Mattancherry, the mosque compound is truly an oasis.

കൽവത്തി പള്ളി

Calvathy Mosque

At the Calvathy Canal, Bazar Road turns to the west and is renamed as it runs along the northern edge of the Cochin peninsula (Calvathy Road). The bridge across the Calvathy canal separated Fort Cochin, which was under British control, from the native ruler's domain. Just past the canal, in what was the European preserve, sits the Calvathy Mosque. The mosque and the nearby canal are the meeting point between the historic European compound of Fort Cochin and the 'native' city, the junction between west and east.

Entrance to Calvathy Canal from the harbour.

Tradition has it that the mosque was built in 1384 to provide a place for prayer for the many Arab traders who came to Cochin. Some say the Arabs built it, some say the local people built it for the Arabs—perhaps two ways of telling the same story. The Calvathy wharf, located on the Calvathy canal south of the mosque, was the site of the old port. This wharf was the principal site of port activity until 1920, when the British created a new port, Willingdon Island, out of the dredgings from deepening the harbour.

T.H. Abdul Khader Moulavi, the present imam of the mosque, believes that the name Calvathy came from the Arabic word *khalwath*, which means no one's place or land. When the Arabs first started coming to trade here, the patch of land that now houses the Calvathy Mosque was literally no one's land. The Arabs camped there while they stayed in Cochin. After some time they decided to build a place for prayer.

Located at the junction between locals and foreigners, the mosque has maintained the tradition of a space where travellers may pray. Besides a variety of traders, Muslims in the British army used the mosque during colonial times. Today, the mosque is home to a large community, with over two thousand participating in Friday prayers. The mosque prides itself on keeping its burial ground open to people of all sects of Islam.

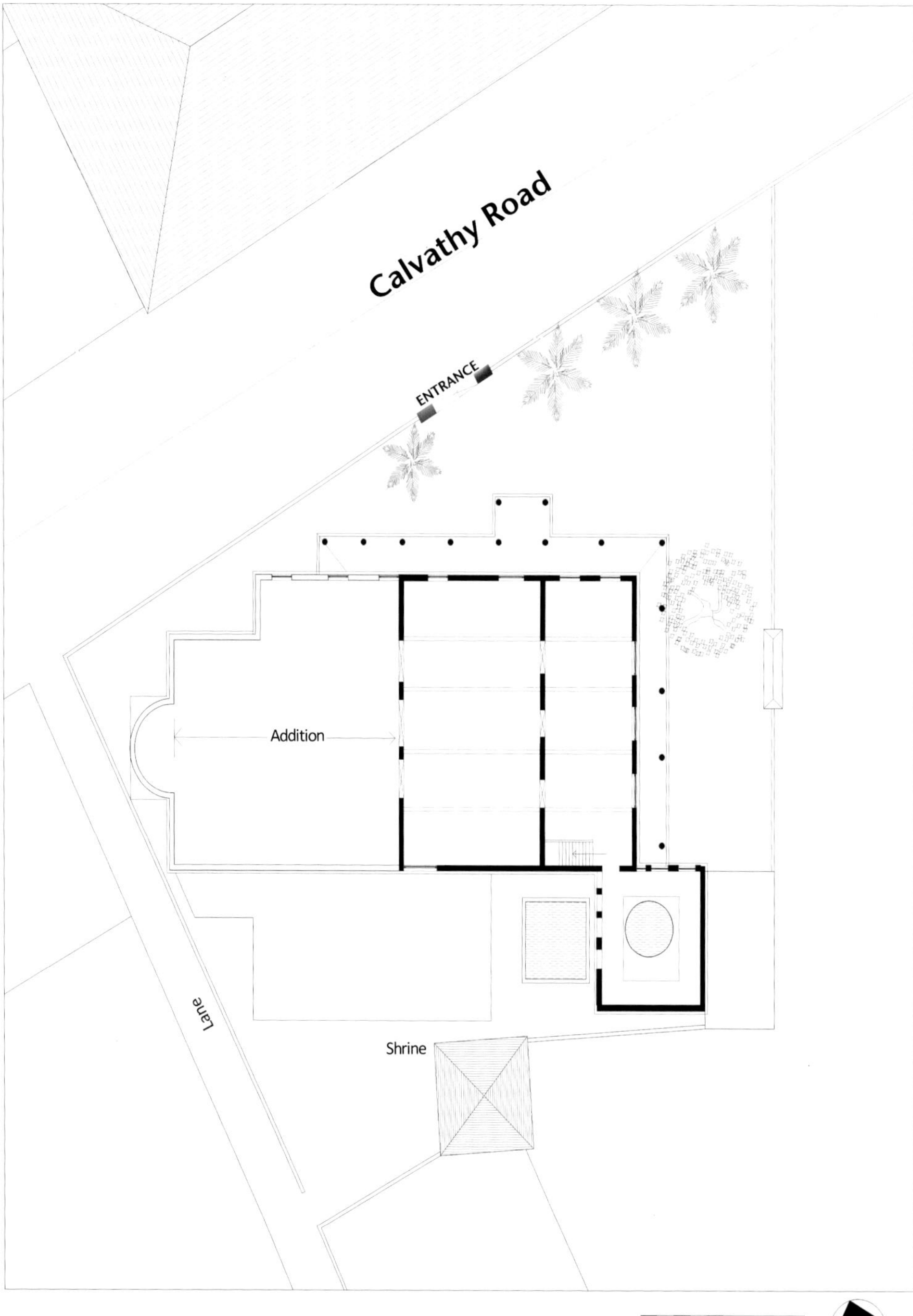

Plan of Calvathy Mosque. Burial space extends to the east and south.

Entry Hall at old mosque.

Calvathy is a mosque of additions, a composition which reflects its long history. An original one-storey mosque with thatched roof was expanded in the late 1800s. A second floor, a third-floor attic and a new tile roof were added. Today, the attic, like so many attics, is full of the cast-offs of centuries, including a visible chronicle of time-telling and lighting devices. The ground floor prayer hall may be the fourteenth-century hall. The original prayer hall and entry hall are of modest size, graced with fine proportions. The beams and ceiling, along with the top floors appear to be products of the nineteenth-century mosque. This expansion was sponsored by Makkar, a successful merchant from Malapuram district (Parapanangadi). A carved board above the door states that the work began at the beginning of the *hijra* year and was finished by year's end.

A major expansion to the mosque took place in 2004–05. The *qibla* wall was removed and the prayer hall extended with a sizeable addition. A large new niche, the *mihrab*, can be seen from the exterior. The top floor of the addition has been opened up to the original second storey and now both are available for the Friday prayer. The single-storey veranda that circled the original prayer hall was removed and a concrete imitation of the wood framed colonnade was built.

The mosque had a generous ablution pool to the south of the entry hall, with a healthy population of fish. The pool is a remnant of the past and seldom used since modern washing

Gate and wall on Calvathy Road. A large donation (collection) box is built into the wall. The old mosque is to the left with the new addition on the right.

facilities, including a stand-up fountain, were built during the renovation. The pool sits between the old mosque and a shrine containing the grave of Faridudeen (Fariduddin) Aulia. The tomb lies in a typical Kerala two-storey structure. Aulia, another of the famous travelling Sufi scholars, died about eighty-five years ago. Friends of the scholar built the structure for his tomb, which continues to receive visitors.

The large compound has a perimeter wall and decorated entry gate facing the main road. The extensive open space to the south and east is used for burial. This space has an impressive variety of trees, many of which were planted during the 1950s by the much revered imam, Marohan Mohammed Ali Musaliar. The present imam, Marohan's successor, has cared for the trees and planted more. The garden includes the ubiquitous coconut palms, bananas and mangoes, along with the more exotic tamarind, teak, jackfruit, nut, banyan and neem (*aryavape*) trees. There is a long tradition in the Middle East of royal gardens planted to reflect paradise. How fitting that here, adjacent to the dusty hectic road, a little bit of paradise reigns in the community burial ground.

ചക്കരയിടുക്ക് ജുമ: മസ്ജിത്

Chakarayidukku Juma Masjid—Eravely Juma Masjid

Malayalam: Chakara (jaggery/sugar) Idukku (small lane/road)

Located a block from Bazar Road on a street that used to favour jaggery[2] merchants, this mosque sits at the intersection of three streets. A red memorial at the junction marks where four Communist Party sympathisers were shot down in 1953 by the local police for holding a political rally.

Chakarayidukku does not have a grand compound. Although hemmed in on all sides, a coconut palm still graces the streetside entry. The mosque is privately owned and was constructed by Ali Kutty, a merchant. Not much is known about Kutty except that his family

2 Unrefined sugar from the sugarcane plant, an important ingredient in south Indian cooking.

came from the north and settled in Cochin. In 1928 a document was registered to establish the on-going maintenance of the mosque by the Kutty family. The 1928 document verifies existence by that date, construction could have been anywhere from twenty to fifty years prior. The present muthavalli, P.M. Abdussamad, is a descendent of Ali Kutty. Although committed to supporting the mosque, the meager rents from shops on the mosque property are not sufficient. He hopes to find new ways to generate income for needed repairs.

The former mayor of Cochin, eighty-four year old T.M. Aboo, resides one block from the mosque. He tells the story he heard about the founding of the mosque.

"The market on Bazar Road was a bustling cosmopolitan place, full of many types of merchants trading everything from gold to coconuts. The founder of the mosque had a

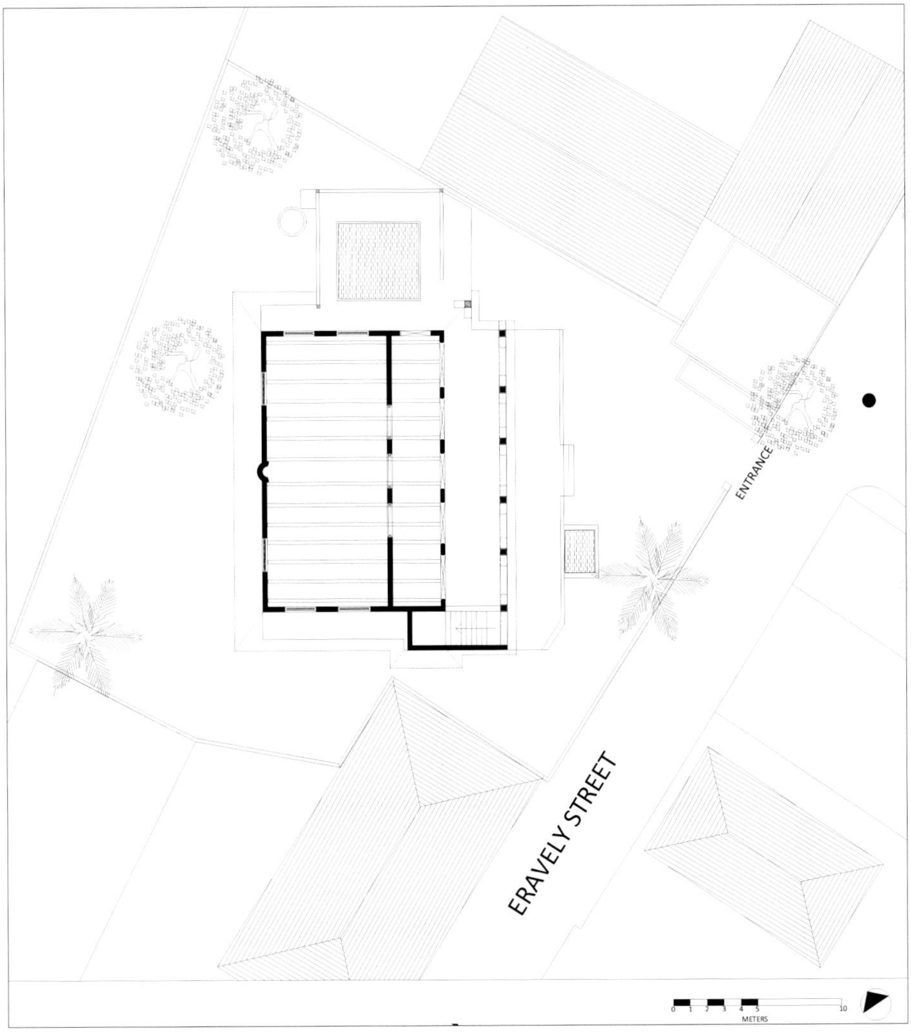

Plan of Chakarayidukku.

Roof top view of Chakarayidukku.

small stall selling vegetables, surrounded by many wealthy traders, most of whom were Gujaratis of either the Muslim or Hindu faith. These Gujaratis lived on the second floor, above their stores on Bazar Road. The ground-floor godowns held all their goods. One midnight there was a big fire and since there was at that time no fire department, all the traders came out to fight the fire. The smaller merchants, like the mosque founder, did not live on Bazar Road but they came as quickly as they could to help put out the fire. The next day, as the founder was trying to salvage whatever was left of his shop he noticed something very shiny. He looked around to see if anyone else had noticed and when no one was looking he took another look. What he found was melted gold from the Gujarati trader upstairs. The fire had caused the gold to liquefy and run down the wall. Now it was buried under the rubble of the shop. The trader, supposedly Ali Kutty, felt the gold was a gift from God so he used the money to make the Haj to Mecca and to build Chakarayidukku. At that time there were not many Muslims residing in that particular area so Kutty spread the word and more people arrived to settle around the mosque."

The two-storey mosque that Ali Kutty built has all the trademark identifiers of Kerala vernacular. The large hipped roof stands above the crowded neighbourhood and a fanciful carved gable faces southwest. The floor plan presents a series of long rectangles, beginning with an insubstantial porch which must have been added recently, not even having a tile roof.

Ablution pool.

Stairs leading to the second floor.

Prayer hall.

The mosque proper opens with six granite pillars framing the three-and-half-metre wide outer veranda. These columns with alternating square and octagonal sections are typical of south Indian pillars from the sixteenth century. It is not clear if the columns were recycled or were made new for the mosque. Wooden capitals top the columns, providing the transition to the timber beam which supports carved rafters. A thin veranda continues around the other three sides of the mosque. Brackets, similar to those at the Cutchi mosque, support the roof. Many have disintegrated and the back veranda has collapsed. Plans are underway to replace the side and rear verandas.

Gate at Eravely Street.

The entry porch forms the next rectangular space; its outer edge marks the wall line of the two-storey structure. An eclectic collection of five arches (see pp. 6–7)welcomes the faithful: the large middle arch is a three leafed cusped arch, the two adjacent are semicircular, and the two end arches are ogee variants of the Mughal arch. A staircase to the south provides access to the second floor which is used for Friday prayer. Similar to the Cutchi and Calvathy mosques, openings in the floor boards allowed everyone to hear the imam before the days of microphones. The prayer hall is reached through three large openings, each with double doors. The middle opening has a beautifully carved wood ensemble of doors and frame. Granite sills grace all the doors. Original glass bell jars and candelabra, similar to those at the Cutchi mosque, hang from the prayer hall beams along with an array of ceiling fans and the much more mundane fluorescent fixture.

A five-metre-square ablution pool sits on the northeast side. The mosque is well used and at Friday prayer up to a thousand men overflow the main hall, the upper floor and all the porches. Fishermen and head carriers say their prayers here along with merchants, government employees, and shop keepers. As the men shed their shoes and perform their ritual ablutions, they physically and symbolically move from the bustle of the secular street to the spiritual serenity of the mosque.

Conclusion
CONSERVATION AS A PART OF THE TWENTY-FIRST CENTURY CITY

"People who come to Kerala almost invariably express delight in its architectural styles. Until a few years ago each town had its own distinctive character... But what have we done in the second half of the twentieth century? Is there any new town in Kerala, or any new part of a town in Kerala which is now worth going to see for its strength of character or beauty? ... All that one can see today is a growing hotch-potch of many-storey buildings in the so-called 'modern' style."

Laurie Baker

"Who in the whole of India cares two paisa about heirlooms if he's given the choice between old stuff and money in the bank?"

Salman Rushdie

The vast majority of worshippers at a Kerala mosque seldom reflect on their mosque as architecture. The act of communal prayer centres their thoughts regarding the local mosque. Unfortunately, it is only once a mosque has disappeared that the community remembers the value of the building. Then there is talk about the spaciousness of the hall, the coolness of the space, the richness of the wood, the treasured feel of the place. Although the people of Kerala conscientiously honour their traditions in religion, dance and music, the building arts have largely been ignored.

Until the twentieth century, the mosques of Kerala reflected the local vernacular. From the first prayer hall raised at Cranganore in the ninth century to the early-twentieth century mosque at Chakarayidukku in Cochin, the means of construction and materials were consistent. Over the years, glazed windows arrived, timber sizes were modified, roofing products evolved, and additions were constructed, but the basics remained unchanged. After World War II and Indian Independence, the populace emphatically welcomed the new: their new country, and with it a new economy, new technology, and new cities. Modern architecture was optimistically promoted. But with time, the global marketplace trivialised modernism with a plethora of cheap materials and poorly thought-out designs. Mosque design turned outward from the tropical splendours of Kerala and began to mimic the styles of Persia, north India, Arabia and beyond. With the introduction of a new look, the climate and customs of Kerala were forgotten.

Left: Old mosque with a sign asking for donations for 'maintenance and renovation'.
Right: A new mosque in the old quarter of Cochin.

This was not a phenomenon exclusive to Kerala, but a universal embracing of the modern style—a style for all, specific to none.

Considering the pace of urban growth and development in India, the mosques of Cochin are vulnerable not only to demolition[1] but also to the loss of their surroundings. The art of conservation is not widely practiced these days, nor are buildings seen in a larger context which acknowledges the role of neighbouring environs, from the palm-treed property and outbuildings of the mosque to the surrounding houses and shops. Protecting the mosque requires looking outside the stone perimeter walls. Context is important for conservation on two levels. First, the ongoing viability of the mosque is directly related to the stability of the neighbourhood. The mosque cannot stand alone—it needs a community for financial support and for the men's presence at prayer. Change is necessary, but there is no reason why Mattancherry and Kochangadi cannot thrive and adapt to contemporary life while utilising a combination of new and old building stock. Second, if nothing is being maintained, and everything is new, the culture of conservation becomes an irrelevant unknown.

Heat, moisture and the extremes of the monsoon deteriorate building materials, and so it is that tropical architecture has always depended on regular renewal. In the days of the

1 Throughout India historic building losses occur daily. For example, experts have estimated that over the last ten years the majority of the old Delhi mansions and havelis have been destroyed. In Pondicherry 500 historic buildings have been demolished over the last five years.

mud hut a family needed to redo the thatch roof annually or biannually. Once plastered walls of stone came into use, they had to be painted and repaired after every monsoon season or the mould blackened them. The impermanence of materials necessitated an ongoing system of maintenance. Historic photographs of Indian cities display well-maintained buildings, but today the concept of keeping up old structures appears to have been forgotten. Now, there are countless roofless buildings, mouldy walls and overgrown gardens. As the old crumbles, the new grows and rapidly deteriorates, to be followed by a newer new. Limited lifespan has become a mantra of the modern age.

Local citizens say that at least half of the old mosques in Cochin have been demolished. Religious leaders felt that difficulties with plastered walls, moisture, toilets, and roof maintenance could only be solved with a new building. Some of the vernacular mosques have been maintained, but the many demolished and altered mosques tell a different story. For the last fifty years Kerala natives have been working in the Arabian Gulf states. Upon return they often give large donations to their local mosque—as an act of devotion and to publicly show that their years of work brought rewards. These funds (and funders) encouraged new construction, either as an addition or a completely new mosque. Old mosques, such as that at Akathe Palli, were torn down and replaced with uninspiring structures.

Additions to old Kerala mosques have seldom complemented the existing structures. New interventions get layered onto the graciously proportioned halls. Domes, minarets,

Kerala street scene, early twentieth century.

concrete columns and flat roofs surround the old masterpiece with scant attention to proportion or integrity.

Centuries-old mosques are now often wrapped in modern kitsch. The structure at Cranganore, which may be the oldest standing mosque in India, has been totally encased in concrete additions, with only a portion of the old roof peeking out. The congregations at both Chembitta Palli and Calvathy attempted to preserve their original mosque, but simply could not resist final touches which added jarring elements to the composition. The Juma Masjid at Ponnani has generations of additions, each one in a different style, each one using different materials, and sadly, each one further cutting off the view of the majestic entrance. Obviously, the builder-funders wanted to imitate the 'famous' mosques. Too often the vernacular mosques are seen as deficient in a perceived Islamic pedigree; the great rain-shedding roofs and distinguished prayer halls remain vastly under-appreciated.

It is murmured that the old mosques look too much like temples; thus they should be dismantled for an 'Islamic' replacement, with a minaret added, of course. A three-hundred-year-old prayer hall is a venerable site. It has borne witness to a multitude of very human concerns. The time is long overdue to celebrate and acknowledge the role of these places. The old mosques of Kerala continue an ancient and powerful relationship of home to house of prayer. Never having put to words the importance of a specific mosque, the faithful should be strongly encouraged to find the vocabulary to express their fondness for a place before it is torn down. The surviving vernacular mosques are outstanding examples of age-old traditions, all the more remarkable because they are a living heritage which is still functional, dynamic, and in daily use.

Looking out over Bazar Road or Kochangadi today, palm trees punctuate the landscape, interspersed with tiled roof structures. These roofs established a rhythm which is slowly being lost to the new flat-roofed insertions. The indigenous mosques have tall ceilings, natural cooling, and a quality of craftsmanship unknown today. The new structures have little relationship to the local climate. Low-ceilinged air conditioned spaces turn into broilers when the daily power outages hit. A generally poor manipulation of materials indicates a problem that is not unique to the modern mosques, but one universally shared with many newly constructed buildings.

In Cochin, funds for maintenance of mosques come from a unique system of management. Each mosque is run either by a committee or, in the case of many of the family mosques documented in this book, by descendents of the mosque's ancestral founder. Mosques often have collection boxes, proceeds of which help fund their upkeep, or they depend on rent from properties adjacent to the mosque or in the vicinity. These properties form a religious endowment (or *waqf*) which the founders set aside for the benefit of the mosque. Each mosque independently hires its own imam. Contact with the *Waqf* Board in Ernakulam—the larger governing body—is minimal and usually only occurs when there is a dispute. Thus, the mosques rely on the whims of succession and local economies for their future.

Since the mosque's maintenance is dependent on rents and donations, the strong support of the community is a must. Unfortunately, Mattancherry is being left to the vagaries of weather, squatters, tourism and random development. Many of the godowns lining Bazar Road have been abandoned as businesses relocated. Those still standing are seen by owners or developers in terms of a future use dedicated to tourism—as guesthouse, restaurant or tourist shop. Other possibilities inherent in a lengthy waterfront, large open structures prime for adaptive reuse, and a resident population of educated workers have been ignored. Options such as an updated spice trade, electronic trading, a renewal of water dependent activity, and service-oriented businesses continue to be unexplored.

Cochin's city fathers are focusing all new development to the east of the city, swallowing up former rice fields.[2] Uncontrolled sprawl with its accompanied reliance on new roadways is the order of the day, even though actual population growth is minimal. As a 2008 headline in *The Hindu* shouted: 'Building a new and resurgent Kochi'. The limited funds for infrastructure, along with business owners seeking expansion space, are directed towards vacant fields. Instead of utilising the pre-existent built-up environment by integrating new structures, rehabilitating old ones and updating services, sprawl invades the countryside.

With property speculation the most recent face of globalisation, old vernacular buildings—home-grown, and certainly the original, 'green' architecture—are being sacrificed throughout Asia. Instead of domestic bricks, timber and stone, buildings are assembled with concrete, steel and imported materials. The use of new and old local materials along with the 'recycling' of existing buildings would more honestly reflect the shortage of many materials and the rapid depletion of fossil fuels. With re-use of existing structures, the demand for concrete[3], aluminum, and steel would lessen, along with the amount of energy required for their manufacture. The arrival of reinforced concrete throughout Asia has brought an impersonal new way of building which promotes increased detachment from place. It has brought very few innovations and much imitation of modern architecture. Glass panels and air-conditioning have created temporary amnesia about the location of these buildings and the woefully deficient electrical supply. Sustainability, use of local materials, and environmentally sensitive design are commendable and much discussed in international architecture journals, but practiced by few, in the West and the East. A city can never be sustainable as long as the built environment is perpetually cast aside to make way for the new.

2 According to the Thiruvananthapuram-based Centre for Development Studies, there has been a 65% decrease in paddy cultivation in the last thirty years.

3 The production of cement (the key ingredient in concrete) is one of the three main contributors to carbon dioxide emissions (the first is burning fossil fuel, the second gas flaring). Saving existing buildings means less use of new concrete.

The glamour of the new is incessantly portrayed by the media, shown in film, on TV and in magazines. Indians are bombarded with images of shiny clean things. No one could be blamed for associating the old with poverty, dirt, and backwardness. Yet, the old may very well offer greater riches than the new; the old may be better built than the tawdry newness which can quickly descend into appalling ugliness. Protecting existing buildings does not mean sinking into a backwards traditionalism; instead it can be a hopeful marshalling of resources for the future. European cities are full of densely packed neighbourhoods made up of seventeenth- or eighteenth-century buildings. But that does not mean that they are cities of the past. Contemporary cities can embrace both the past and the future. Some are now saying that a city of the future will not even have the highways of the twentieth-century metropolis, but instead be a grid of public transport and pedestrian amenities. In Cochin, the future could bring renewed use of the myriad waterways as the system of transport. Old buildings (and alternative forms of transport) could become as much a part of the city of the future as the internet or touch-screen technology.

The public may romanticise old buildings, speaking fondly of them, but this is mostly done in the past tense. The people's relationship with the Kerala vernacular is deep-seated and intimate. But it has been difficult to extend that feeling to a public discussion about the myriad possibilities to be found in the existing building stock. The need for more housing is talked about as if the existing housing did not count.[4] Hi-rise density is discussed without considering the density possible with narrow streets and a non-car dependent lifestyle.[5] The lanes of Kochangadi can be a model for a liveable city of the future, not a blank slate for new housing. New construction is often draped with concrete copies of the trademark Kerala roof, plaster replicas of columns, or concrete beams decorated to look like wood. Meanwhile, old buildings with ancient teak beams, irreplaceable timber roofs, and fine carvings are being taken down. Old structures are recycled into tourist villages or sold in pieces to the wealthy for decoration. As badly-built structures rise, examples of the fine craftsmanship of Indian artisans are being transported worldwide for the antique market.

After years of detachment from the street-level reality of cities, the guardian of India's artistic legacy, the Indian Trust for Art and Cultural Heritage (INTACH), has become aware that India is rapidly losing its patrimony. The INTACH charter of 2004 clearly states the need for recognition of vernacular buildings and historic settlements. The "majority of architectural properties and sites in India still remains unidentified, unclassified, and unprotected..."

---

4 For sure, slums are an extreme problem in India, but solid buildings constructed a hundred years ago, then allowed to decay and house myriad families, are not in the same category as slum housing built over the last twenty years, although government reports often lack any discrimination between the two.

5 The highest population densities in greater Kochi are on peninsular Cochin, not multi-storeyed Ernakulam. Although much of the housing is sub-standard and needs upgrading, large numbers of solid structures remain.

Abandoned building along the Cochin waterfront.

The charter perceptively and creatively lists alternative methods for conservation, such as utilising indigenous building traditions and recognising 'master builders'. A conversation has started about the need to abandon the strict rules of Western preservation and look to an Indian version of conservation for the masses of vernacular buildings. But, so far, few seem to be taking up the mandate. An INTACH report on Fort Cochin/Mattancherry reiterated the need for protection of the entire area, but it has been gathering dust on the shelf for over a decade. The mosques of Cochin are not even mentioned in the report.

The Indian government, already dealing with so many monuments, regards historic preservation as entombment, a literal 'preservation' of the monumental, not a process of conserving buildings for an ongoing role in the twenty-first century city. This philosophy may be a result of the founding history of the Archaeological Survey of India (ASI), the other guardian of India's heritage, set up by the British in 1861. Norman O. Brown, in his classic *Life Against Death,* theorised that institutions take on the personalities of their founders, their histories and their neuroses. The British were deeply disturbed by the sense of disorder in Indian cities. Their solution was to clear the space around monuments, effectively removing the living connection to the city. Even today, monuments in India are typically surrounded by an English-style lawn.

Niche with prayer books at Ponnani Juma Masjid.

On the dry plains of central Karnataka, the 'ruins'—the ones deemed worthy of preserving—of the Vijayanagara capital city are picture perfect, with green grass set against the rocky landscape and few remnants of what was once a teeming city.

In his two volume *History of Indian and Eastern Architecture,* written in 1876, James Fergusson was passionate about the architecture of India. But he ignored the beautiful courtyard houses, the sophisticated water systems or any of the functional vernacular. Typical of Englishmen at the time, he focused on monuments that met his aesthetic sensibilities, ignoring the chaotic civil life of India. In the twenty-first century, traditional urban architecture still lacks recognition. India has such an historical wealth of monuments that a distorted view of what constitutes the architectural has resulted. The contextual fabric for many of the nation's great monuments—the houses, shops, the entire urban setting built in a sympathetic scale and often of similar materials—is rapidly disappearing or already gone.

Waiting for the 'other' (government or tourism) to do conservation work has led to the decay of myriad historic buildings in the private sector. Examples of renovations that highlight the potential and integrity of old buildings are few. In Cochin, the vast majority of restorations have been connected to tourism and have not provided a renewal of workplaces and homes for the local population. While this work is to be commended, affordable restoration and maintenance procedures need to be a part of the lives of all.

Since a pattern of consistent neglect reigns, from government facilities to two-room homes, a renewed philosophy of maintaining a city's building stock is essential if anything is to remain of India's past. Citizens, religious institutions and businesses involved in renovations need a simple set of standards, including information on proper window and door treatments, wood preservatives, and the technologies of brick with plaster walls, tile roofs, and concrete floors. The labour force could increase its technical capabilities with apprentices in the long-held building skills of plastering, wood-working and stone work. A rekindled interest in local materials would focus attention on the beauty of the old screens, shutters, eaves and doors; the artistry of traditional lime plaster which has a more subtle and elegant look and feel than the new cement plasters; the design of airy rooms and courtyards. Although India has no shortage of manpower, artisans have been marginalised (or ignored) in the present construction scenario. In order for a reinvigorated class of master craftsmen to flourish, young apprentices need to be united with senior masters. Otherwise, the knowledge learned from centuries of manipulating local materials will be entirely lost. The leaders at Chembitta Palli found it difficult to find a carpenter who understood the carving and joinery necessary to replace one wooden column.

There are countless reasons to conserve. But nothing will happen until individual property owners see value in their building. Besides the arguments of social and cultural values and sustainability, the beneficial economics of ongoing maintenance need to be further substantiated. Conservation protects an investment, instead of allowing it to waste away. Who is to lead this endeavour? Organisations like INTACH need a broader base, their efforts expanded to include the media, local social activists, and environmental organisations. To date, activists in India have focused on the natural environment or artistic heritage. INTACH could lead the way in incorporating building heritage into the activist's lexicon. With federal level grants INTACH could partner with construction trade organisations to create a maintenance/restoration manual and craftsman education programs.

Government will only respond when political will is galvanised into action by the citizenry. Politicians need to be won over to the positive values of conservation. The voices of an educated citizenry and energised conservation organisations can publicise examples of affordable rehabilitations, the profitability of cultural tourism, and the real-life balance sheet of sustainable action. To ensure that valued existing buildings remain a part of the old city, local governments must establish basic parametres for development. Zoning regulations and tax advantages for conserving the buildings of the old city are a first step. Presently, planning in the greater Kochi area is sketchy or non-existent. City planners have minimal documentation of the extant buildings of Mattancherry. Surveys show several Hindu temples, the Jewish synagogue and the Raja's palace, but there is no mention of the old mosques or the many substantial godowns. The official conservation zone includes only the colonial settlement.

Typically, regulations that are on the books are ignored and enforcement is rare. Stabilising land values is key to protecting existing buildings. Property value is directly related to development potential. If ten-storey development is allowed where two- and three-storey buildings now stand, the economic incentive forces demolition. In the West, even religious buildings have been the victim of the wrecking ball as congregations sell out when land values become exorbitant, usually as a result of increased height allowances.

Everywhere around the world, every generation erases a bit of the collective past, convinced that they have a better way to build. While one and all applaud India's economic advancement and development, does it have to be at the expense of India's entire history? The neglect of the old cities of India has reached epidemic proportions. In a time of rapid change, there is even more need for permanence, a need which can be met by keeping the old city centres alive. For parts of Cochin, the mosques, which hold a place of respect and honour in the community, can be a catalyst for new thinking, leading the way in demonstrating the possibilities of continued life for existing buildings.

On the shores of the Arabian Sea, Malayalees practicing the major faiths of the world have resided together for centuries. In these times of religious segregation the Cochin mosque provides a powerful reminder of the longstanding peaceful assimilation of Islam into the life of Kerala. Historically, periods of cooperation brought prosperity to all the people on the Malabar Coast. Sadly, the colonialists, and later the fundamentalists (of all faiths), eroded this enlightened fabric of life. Working together, Indians can be a major force in the twenty-first century, or they can fight amongst themselves—especially about the dangerous emotional issues of religion—and lose their chance at greatness. Bearing witness with their magnificent presence, the old mosques can strike a vital chord of memory. Respectful coexistence has been and should continue to be a fundamental part of daily life.

In the broader panorama of the Asian trading networks, the tropical mosque is a unique byproduct—a physical reminder of what was once a complex set of international mercantile connections that thrived without telegraph, telephone or internet. Islam served as a unifying force for large-scale commercial trade and created a chain of caravan and maritime routes which joined far-off ports on the Indian Ocean to the Mediterranean. But, travel anywhere in the southern lands of Asia today and it will be quickly evident that physical evidence of this illustrious chapter of history has almost completely vanished. Throughout the coastal monsoon zone, a roof-dominated architecture developed. Often tiered and with open colonnades, these grand tropical structures served the needs of royalty, religion and residents. The old mosques were a key part of this architecture, displaying the abundance of solid timber and the skill of the builders. Today, these structures could be put on the endangered species list—if such a category existed. In Malaysia and Indonesia, oil wealth has brought replacement mosques that—like the new structures in Kerala—have little to do with local history, climate, or customs. The ancient mosques of Cambodia and Vietnam are also gone; victims of war, neglect and replacement. Although the present text highlights six mosques in one area of Cochin, their presence should not be taken as evidence of secure historic buildings. It is a quirk of history and economics that so many have survived in Cochin; in most of tropical Asia, the mosques of centuries past have completely disappeared.

A vernacular mosque seen through the tropical palms of Kerala.

Boys on their way to the mosque to celebrate Bakrid.

ACKNOWLEDGEMENTS

I first studied Islamic architecture while attending architecture school at the University of California, Berkeley. I dreamed of visiting the great stone mosques of Isfahan, Cairo and Istanbul. Little could I have imagined that I would become an advocate for the dreamy, sleepy, timber-roofed mosques of tropical Asia. In 1992–94 I found myself working for the mayor of Penang, Malaysia on a conservation plan for the historic old centre of Penang. A multi-ethnic community—Chinese, Malay and Indian—lives and works there. Collaborating with Khoo Su Nin, now known as Khoo Salma Nasution, a brilliant young historian and writer, the old city was documented and conservation guidelines created. One of my favourite buildings was a timber-roofed airy mosque built by the traders from Aceh in Sumatra.

It may be that my happy childhood in New Orleans, land of swamps, heat, rain and bugs, predisposed me to a love of decaying buildings in tropical climates. In 2004 my artist husband was awarded a Fulbright Scholars Grant for a project on pepper and trade. During our two-year stay in Cochin I researched building conservation in Kerala, and the idea for this book began to take shape. Walking the city and talking to architects, citizens, preservationists, developers, city planners, and politicians I realised that the rich vernacular of the old trading city was mostly demeaned or ignored. There was a particular wealth of mosques that especially intrigued me. One of the people I met was a former city councilor, M. Iqbal. Over countless glasses of tea and morning discussions, he guided me through the ins and outs of the local community. In Malaysia I had benefited from a similar mentor, Muhammad, a former school principal, who was officially my Malay teacher but took it upon himself to explain in great detail the precepts of Islam. Iqbal took me through the sects and sub-sects of Kerala. With the help of Jiju, a young man of Mattancherry who also assisted my husband, I began exploring the back streets and visiting mosques. Iqbal encouraged me to apply for grants so that a book could be published about this amazing—but unknown—resource. With the cooperation of Dr Rajan Chedembath of Cochin's Centre for Heritage, Environment and Development, we received a Ford Foundation Grant. Thanks to the grant I was able to return in 2007–08 to finish my research.

Portions of the first chapters appeared in an article in the Fall 2006 issue of *PLACES*. Much of my academic research was carried out at the University of Washington library. I am very grateful for the use of this outstanding institution and the wide selection of books has been an enormous help. But, I have purposely tried to keep this book accessible to the general public. All the academic tomes in the library cannot help if the public fails to appreciate these fine buildings. After thirty years of conservation work I know that unless the man on the street is convinced of the value of a building, all the fine studies and research are to naught. I fervently hope that this book will not turn out to be a document of lost assets but will remain a celebration of living structures.

I wish to thank all the people of Mattancherry who told me their stories, smiled as I bicycled by, and shared with me their houses of prayer. The following are a few:
At the mosques, I am indebted to A.S. Abdul Latheef Sait (Cutchi Hanafi Mosque), Abdul Koya, Zainudheen Naina, and Al-Haj K.K. Abdul Rahiman Moulavi, (Chembitta Palli), P.M. Abdussamad, Abdul Rathman Haji, and Mohiyadeen P.M. Abdul Majeedh (Chakarayidukku), Haji Kutty Naina (Mammu Surka), Hashim Kochukoya Thangel (Thakyavu Palli), A.K. Raja Anwar and T.H. Abdul Khader Moulavi (Calvathy), Makhdoom Sayed Muthu Koyathangal and T.K. Mohamed (Ponnani). Friends in Kerala who offered insights and encouragement include Dorrie Younger and Anoop Skaria, Javeed Hashim, Manoj Kini, A. Kutbudin, Ramla Babu, Mayor Mercy Williams, Corporation of Cochin, Abul Kalam Azad, Rajan Chedembath, Soya Parammel, T.M. Aboo, and Krishnan Nair Studio.

This project would not have had its successful outcome without the help of Jane Schukoske, Fulbright India and Ganesan Balachander, Ford Foundation, New Delhi. Mehrdad Shokoohy, who wrote the first and only English language book focused on the south Indian mosques, was generous in his assistance and his encouragement of this work. Needed hands for measuring and mapping were provided by Pramod and Vinil in Cochin and Shweta Bhatia Gupta in Seattle. Sebastian Prange helped with Arabic translations. Bipin Shah of Mapin Publishing was an ever-present source of support. In Seattle, Manish Chalana, Cathy Hillenbrand, Annie Grosshans, and Gary Hamilton provided local sustenance. Finally, I thank my son Benjamin for poetic inspiration and Swami, for initiating our own quest for pepper.

NOTE:

Transliterated terms adopted from the original language (e.g. Malayalam or Arabic) are generally spelled without diacritical signs. Words in Malayalam in general use are treated as normal, while those in Arabic are in italics. Malayalam words or names are found in slightly varying forms in English. I have tried to note the most common current English spelling used in Kerala. In a city and region where names and spellings of names change monthly or yearly, it is difficult to have a 'definitive' English spelling. Often the term in common use in Kerala is different from that used in other parts of India. For the mosque name I have used the most common term, even though this leads to some mosques being labeled as 'masjid' and others as 'palli'.

Malayalam has an extensive vocabulary for building parts, as well as for the procedures of building. Although these Malayalam words are quite beautiful I have tried to use more common words to reduce confusion for non-Malayalee readers.

TEAM

Without this group the book would not have been possible. Feroze, besides being a fine photographer and an enthusiastic participant, offered help with everything from computer glitches to social mores. Jiju was translator, assistant, go-between, informant and all around resource for the life of Mattancherry. I can't thank Feroze and Jiju enough for their willingness to share their knowledge and help shape this book. My husband was occupied with another project in Cochin, but offered to help in photographing the mosques so that I was free to interview leaders, sketch and measure the buildings, and take in the environs. His artist eye gives another perspective on the mosques.

Feroze Babu is a lifetime resident of Cochin. Feroze was chief photographer for the Malayalam Manorama (the largest circulated newspaper in India) for twelve years. He has received numerous awards for his photographs and his work in photojournalism.

Donald Fels, an artist, has taken photographs for decades, sometimes as part of his multi-media pieces, often as a source for paintings. Since 2003, he has been creating a series of metal billboard paintings with south Indian billboard painters. The touring exhibition, *What is a Trade?* employs the billboard paintings to examine the legacy of Vasco da Gama.

Patricia Tusa Fels is an architect and conservationist. She has been involved in conservation projects in the U.S., Italy and Malaysia for the last thirty years. In addition to a lengthy career in architecture, she has written articles for a wide range of journals and newspapers.

Mohammed Yousuf Jiju was born and raised in Mattancherry. A natural linguist, he speaks Malayalam, Hindi, English, and Tamil, and some Arabic. He has just completed his Bachelor's degree in history and hopes to pursue a Master's degree in journalism.

BIBILIOGRAPHY

Abdurrahman, K.V. *Brief Stories about the Mappila History*. Ponnani: Muslim Service Society, 1998.

Rahim, Abdur Khawaja, ed. *Iqbal, the Poet of Tomorrow*. Lahore: Abdul Hameed Khan at Ferozsons Ltd, 1968.

Alfieri, Binaca Maria. *Islamic Architecture of the Indian Subcontinent*. London: Laurence King, 2000.

Appleyard, Donald, ed. *The Conservation of European Cities*. Cambridge, Mass: The MIT Press, 1979.

Engineer, Asghar Ali, ed. *Kerala Muslims: A Historical Perspective*. New Delhi: Ajanta Publications, 1995.

Asher, Catherine, and Cynthia Talbot. *India before Europe*. New York: Cambridge University Press, 2006.

Ballhatchet, Kenneth, and David Taylor, eds. *Changing South Asia: City and Culture*. Hong Kong: Asian Research Service, 1984.

Bastea, Eleni, ed. *Memory and Architecture*. Albuquerque: University of New Mexico Press, 2004.

Bayly, Susan. *Saints, Goddesses and Kings*. Cambridge: Cambridge University Press, 1989.

Bhatia, Gautam. *Laurie Baker: Life Work, Writings*. New Delhi: Penguin Books, 1994.

Boyer, M. Christine. *The City of Collective Memory*. Cambridge, Mass: MIT Press, 1994.

Braudel, Fernand. *A History of Civilizations*. New York: Penguin Press, 1993.

Cantacuzino, Sherban, ed. *Architecture in Continuity: Building in the Islamic World Today*. New York: Aperture, 1985.

Chaudhuri, K.N. *Trade and Civilisation in the Indian Ocean*. Cambridge: Cambridge University Press, 1985.

———. *Asia Before Europe*. Cambridge: Cambridge University Press, 1990.

T.S. Prabhu, Balagopal. "Kerala Architecture." In *Essays on the Cultural Formation of Kerala*, ed. P.J. Cherian. Thiruvananthapuram: Kerala Council for Historical Research, 1999.

Dale, Stephen Frederic. *Islamic Society on the South Asian Frontier: The Mappilas of Malabar*. Oxford: Clarendon Press, 1980.

———. Trade, Conversion and the Growth of the Islamic Community of Kerala, South India. *Studia Islamica*, no. 71 (1990): 155–175.

Day, Francis. *The Land of the Permauls or Cochin: Its Past and Its Present*, 1863. Reprint, New Delhi: Asian Educational Services, 1990.

Dunn, Ross E. *The Adventures of Ibn Battuta—A Muslim Traveler of the 14th Century*. Rev. ed. Berkeley: University of California Press, 2005.

Eaton, Richard M., ed. *India's Islamic Traditions, 711–1750*. New Delhi: Oxford University Press, 2003.

Fergusson, James. *History of Indian and Eastern Architecture*. London: J. Murray, 1910.

Dept of Architecture. *Fort Cochin Mattancherry, A Study of Space and Society*. Trivandrum: Dept of Architecture, 1995–96.

Frishman, Martin, and Hasan-Uddin Khan, eds. *The Mosque*. London: Thames and Hudson, 1994.

Galeano, Eduardo. *Memory of Fire: I. Genesis*. Trans. Cedric Belfrage. New York: Pantheon Books, 1985.

Ghosh, Amitav. *In an Antique Land*. New Delhi: Ravi Dayal Publisher, 1992.

———. *The Iman and the Indian*. New Delhi: Ravi Dayal Publisher, 2002.

Gilmartin, David, and Bruce B. Lawrence, ed. *Beyond Turk and Hindu—Rethinking Religious Identities in Islamicate South Asia*. Gainesville: University Press of Florida, 2000.

Gupta, Anirudhda, ed. *Minorities on India's West Coast.* New Delhi: Kalinga Publications, 1991.

Haidar, Mansura, ed. *Sufis, Sultans and Feudal Orders.* New Delhi: Manohar, 2004.

Horovitz, J. *List of the Published Mohamedan Inscriptions of India. Epigraphia Indo-Moslemica 1909–10.* New Delhi: Archaeological Survey of India, 1987.

Iqbal, Muhammad. *Poems from Iqbal.* Trans. V.G. Kiernan. London: John Murray, 1955.

Katakam, Ramu. *Glimpses of Architecture in Kerala.* New Delhi: Rupa & Co, 2006.

Khan, Ahmad Nabi. *Islamic Architecture in South Asia.* Oxford: Oxford University Press, 2003.

Kittredge, William. *The Nature of Generosity.* New York: Knopf, 2000.

Logan, William. *Malabar Manual.* 2 vols. Reprint, New Delhi: Asian Educational Services, 2000.

Randathani, Husain, ed. *Makdhoomum Ponnaniyum.* Ponnani: Ponnani Juma Masjid Committee, 1998.

Malekandathil, Pius. *Portuguese Cochin and the Maritime Trade of India 1500–1663.* New Delhi: Manohar, 2001.

Malieckal, Bindu. "Muslims, Matriliny, and A Midsummer Night's Dream: European Encounters with the Mapplilas of Malabar, India." *The Muslim World*, no. 95 (April 2005): 297–316.

Mathew, K.S., ed. *Maritime Malabar and The Europeans.* Haryana: Hope India Publications; Kolkata: Maulana Abul Kalam Azad Institute of Asian Studies with IRISH-Meshar, 2003.

Mayaram, Shail, M.S.S. Pandian, and Ajay Skaria, eds. *Muslims, Dalits, and the Fabrications of History.* London: Seagull Books, 2008.

Mehta, R.N. *Champaner, A Mediaeval Capital.* Baroda: Heritage Trust and Archaeological Survey of India, 1986.

Metcalf, Thomas R. *An Imperial Vision.* Berkeley: University of California Press, 1989.

Naipaul, V.S. *Beyond Belief.* London: Little, Brown & Co., 1998.

Nizami, Khaliq Ahmad. *Religion and Politics in India during the 13th Century*, 1961. Reprint, New Delhi: Oxford University Press, 2002.

Pramar, V.S. *A Social History of Indian Architecture.* New Delhi: Oxford University Press, 2005

Prasad, N.Devi. *Fort Cochin & Mattancherry—A Monograph.* New Delhi: INTACH, 1994.

Rushdie, Salman. *The Moor's Last Sigh.* London: Vintage, 1996.

Said, Edward W. *Orientalism.* New York: Vintage Books, 1979.

Samad, Dr M. Abdul. *Islam in Kerala.* Kollam: Laurel Publications, 1998.

Vasudevan, Ravi, Ravi Sundaram, Jeebesh Bagchi, Monica Narula, Geert Lovink, and Shuddhabrata Sengupta, eds. *Sarai Reader 02: The Cities of Everyday Life.* New Delhi: Centre for the Study of Developing Societies, 2002.

Sarkar, H. *Monuments of Kerala.* New Delhi: Archaeological Survey of India, 1992.

Shokoohy, Mehrdad. *Muslim Architecture of South India.* London: RoutledgeCurzon, 2003.

Tillotson, G.H.R., ed. *Paradigms of Indian Architecture.* Richmond, Surrey: Curzon Press, 1998

———. *The Tradition of Indian Architecture.* New Haven and London: Yale University Press, 1989

White, Richard. *The Middle Ground.* Cambridge: Cambridge University Press, 1991

Wolpert, Stanley. *A New History of India*, 5th ed. New York: Oxford University Press, 1997.

Shaykh Zainuddin Makhdum. *Tuhfat al-Mujahidin.* Trans. S. Muhammad Husayn Nainar. Calicut: Other Books, 2006.

Prayer hall at the Juma Masjid of Ponnani. The oil lamp at the centre was supposedly used by Shaikh Zainuddin when he taught students at night. It is still lit nightly.